River *of the* Angry Moon

BELLA COOLA REGION

130°   128°   126°W

0   50   100   km

Skeena R

54°

Ootsa L

Whitesail L

Eutsuk L

Tetachuk L

B R I T I S H

Kitlope

Kimsquit

Dean R

Stuie   ● Anahim Lake

Bella Coola R   Atnarko

●Ocean Falls

Bella
Coola

Hagensborg

●Bella Bella

C O L U M B I A

52°N

52°N

Pacific

Rivers Inlet

Ocean

N

Fort Rupert ●

CANADA

Area
enlarged

U.S.A.

VANCOUVER
ISLAND

128°   126°W

S. DANIEL/STARSHELL MAPS, 1998

River *of the*
Angry Moon

Seasons on the Bella Coola

Mark Hume
with Harvey Thommasen

GREYSTONE BOOKS
Douglas & McIntyre
Vancouver/Toronto

University of Washington Press
Seattle

98 99 00 01 02 5 4 3 2 1

Greystone Books
A division of Douglas & McIntyre Ltd.
1615 Venables Street
Vancouver, British Columbia
V5L 2H1

Canadian Cataloguing in Publication Data
Hume, Mark, 1950–
    River of the Angry Moon

    ISBN 1-55054-660-0
    1. Hume, Mark 1950– 2. Bella Coola River (B.C.) 3. Fly fishing—British
Columbia—Bella Coola River. I. Thommasen, Harvey Victor, 1957– II. Title.
SH572.B8H85 1998   799.1'24'097111   C98-910705-1

Originated by Greystone Books and published simultaneously in the United
States of America by the University of Washington Press, PO BOX 50096, Seattle,
WA 98145-5096.

Library of Congress Cataloging-in-Publication Data
Hume, Mark.
    River of the angry moon : seasons on the Bella Coola / Mark Hume with
Harvey Thommasen

        p.   cm.
    ISBN 0-295-97744-2
    1. Natural history—British Columbia—Bella Coola River. 2. Fly fishing—
British Columbia—Bella Coola River. 3. Seasons—British Columbia—Bella Coola
River. I. Thommasen, Harvey Victor, 1957– . II. Title.
    QH106.2.B8H85   1998   98-26031
    508.711'1—dc21   CIP

Edited by Nancy Flight
Jacket and text design by Isabelle Swiderski
Typesetting by Typographics West
Illustration by Alistair Anderson
Map by S. Daniel/Starshell Maps, 1998
Printed and bound in Canada by Friesens
Printed on acid-free paper ∞

The publisher gratefully acknowledges the support of the Canada Council for the
Arts and of the British Columbia Ministry of Tourism, Small Business and Culture.
The publisher also acknowledges the financial support of the Government of Canada
through the Book Publishing Industry Development Program for its publishing activities.

For Carol and Maggie,
who make coming home from the river worthwhile

Contents

⌢

Prologue

This book was born on the banks of the Bella Coola River. For several years, Harvey Thommasen had been researching the natural history of the valley, where he'd come to live and to work as a family physician. The catalogue of information he'd compiled was staggering. He'd captured and identified hundreds of aquatic insects, memorized sound tapes so that he could recognize birds by their songs, done clinical studies on Native medicinal plants and taken time on his rounds to question elders about the way things had been. He turned river stones, collected mushrooms, pored over scientific papers, compiled detailed field notes and stood for countless hours in the rain watching birds. And of course he spent a lot of time fishing, going out to the river even in the worst weather to see how nature was unfolding—and to try to catch steelhead.

Our friendship, and my curiosity about this great watershed, drew me to the Bella Coola and Atnarko Rivers. As we kayaked and waded from the headwaters to the estuary, we talked about how to best tell the story of this verdant coastal valley. We did not want to write just about fishing—although fish and the river were at the heart of it all—but instead sought to convey the complexity of a temperate rain forest ecosystem of which this river, and others like it, are an integral part. We eventually fixed on the Native calendar of the moons, which in turn is linked to the salmon, to guide us through the forest and into the river.

After the book was started, the Bella Coola was closed to steelhead fishing because stocks had become endangered. So this is a story about loss, about human imperative, about greed and shortsightedness as much as it is about the changing seasons an angler experiences on a wild and beautiful river.

Nature is resilient and salmon are incredibly fecund. The waters should abound with fish. When they do not it is a sign of terrible mismanagement, not by fisheries bureaucrats, but by society as a whole. We believe that a new paradigm is needed on the Pacific coast, one that recognizes the intricate complexity of the rain forest and that limits the excessive killing of salmon so that stocks might recover.

Harvey compiled the research data that are the basis of this book, and he provided detailed field notes of his experiences. I did the writing, based on my own trips to the Bella Coola, and on a lifetime of fishing and wading other coastal rivers in British Columbia. This is not an account of one year on one river, nor is it a story of one angler's observations. At times I saw the river through Harvey's eyes; at times I drew on my own memories of rivers that once were as wild, and of the fish that swam in them. The descriptions of light passing through the forest, of the scent of spring, of the breath of a wolf and of feeling a fish dying in my hands are drawn not from Harvey's careful scientific notes but from my own recurring dreams of rivers. When the manuscript was complete, I honed it, compressed it and polished it, debating the results and conclusions with Harvey. We have strived throughout to produce a book that accurately reflects the passing of the seasons and that captures the mystical experience of fishing a river in the heart of a temperate rain forest. In the end, not certain we could ever finish such a monumental task, we released it with a mixed sense of loss and accomplishment.

We would like to thank Rob Sanders at Greystone Books for his enthusiastic support, based on reading a few draft chapters, and Nancy Flight for her sensitive editing. Carol Thommasen, Al Purkiss and the late Miguel Moreno, provided invaluable critical comment, and Russ Hilland assisted with data, for which we are grateful.

—Mark Hume

January

Angry Moon

The river is fed by the sky. It runs over a bed of shattered mountains, through the dreams of a great forest and into the mouths of ancient fishes. It starts in clouds as grey and heavy as the sea and ends in a windswept estuary haunted by ghosts. It is a place where white swans dance on dark mud flats and salmon lay fragile eggs in nests of stone.

Somewhere fish are dying in the river and somewhere they are beginning, flickers of movement inside orange orbs that must seem to them as large and bright as the sun. Somewhere, lying sedately in the shelter of river boulders, are the wild steelhead, with pale green backs and cheeks flushed with pink. They are waiting for spring—and when you set out to find them, you find many things.

Coming to Bella Coola across the undulating Chilcotin Plateau, you see the mountains rise in the distance, blue and green and smudged with the soft tones of the earth. Pavement turns to dirt as you pass into the shadow of the mountains. The rough road, built not by government but by a community hungry for contact, somehow finds a pathway through the Coast Mountains. It clings to the dizzying slopes and sways me back and forth in my truck as it flows down with gravity. At Young Creek, where the stream has cut a great chasm in the rock, I fall and fall and fall, bewildered by the suddenness of the geography, until I reach the valley floor and bump onto pavement again. It is only when I see the Atnarko River that I get reoriented and realize how tightly I have gripped the wheel. Not far ahead lies the Pacific; I can sense it hanging in the air.

The raw mountains along British Columbia's coast open at Bella Coola into a narrow valley that has been shaped by glaciers and smoothed by the endless flow of water. From Alaska to Oregon there are openings in the mountain wall like this, but most of those places have been beaten down by logging, tamed by urban growth, and the natural movement of water has been halted by dams. This valley is different, for although it has been settled the river within it remains wild, as if in this great folded terrain time itself somehow became trapped. I knew the first time I walked along the river here, tilting my head to catch the scent of grizzly, that this was a special place.

The mountains that surround the Bella Coola River catch the clouds lumbering in off the ocean and transform them from within. As they pass over, adding infinite layers of snow to the ice fields, they wash the lower slopes in heavy rains. An intricate network of streams, ponds, lakes and rivers springs to life, linking the watershed. They spill together, forming the Bella Coola's major tributaries—the Atnarko, which rises from Charlotte Lake on the dry Chilcotin Plateau to lead you into the country, and the Talchako, which is born from a weeping glacier in the Coast Mountains.

The Bella Coola River begins at the point where the two rivers meet. Flowing west, it passes through a tangled forest before entering a sweeping estuary buttressed by a great black wall of stone on the north shore. Here it empties into the churning tidal waters of North Bentinck Arm. Along its course, the Bella Coola is fed by streams that leap and crash towards it from the slopes. Burnt Bridge, Noosgulch, Cacoohtin, Snootli, Thorsen and others pour in, bringing so much of the mountains with them that the river runs the colour of milk in all but the coldest months. Some of these streams flow through places where slabs of smooth rock wear weird hieroglyphic faces—carvings that date back ten thousand years or more. Immutable, troubled faces that like a lot of things in this valley came soon after the glaciers retreated.

Because of the Pacific Ocean, the climate in the Bella Coola Valley is much milder than on the Interior Plateau. There in January the temperature can plummet to -50° C, freezing metal and snapping the will of even the toughest rancher. But on the coast, just a short drive away, the mean temperature for January hovers near zero.

In the valley, rain is more likely than snow even in the coldest month—and it is never long before it rains at any time of the year. It is written into the meteorologic plans for the valley. Bella Coola receives 150 centimetres of rain a year—three times as much water as falls from the sky at Anahim Lake, just to the east in the rain shadow of the Coast Mountains but three times less than the rainfall at Ocean Falls, 64 kilometres to the west. The rain comes as a soft, enveloping drizzle that can go on for weeks at a time, saturating the landscape. Occasionally there is a tremendous deluge: up to 23 centimetres has fallen here in twenty-four hours.

RIVER OF THE ANGRY MOON

The mild climate, long growing season and generous rainfall in the Bella Coola Valley has created a coastal temperate rain forest of stunning richness. Here, as in other valleys in the Pacific Northwest, a dense and luxurious growth of vegetation reaches out and entwines the land. In this verdant jungle plants grow in every available space: on fallen logs, on the bases and branches of large trees, even on the rocks. Here an abandoned truck is camouflaged by mouldering vegetation, devil's club grows in the wheel wells, and alder branches tap the windshield; there an old cabin seems to sag under the weight of grass carpeting its roof. In the forest, curtains of lichen drape the trees and ferns grow so thickly about your legs you can't see the ground you're walking on. Along one side stream you can peel back slabs of moss to find where Nuxalk artists imprinted the faces and symbols of hundreds of spirits in timeless stone, only to have the patient forest draw its veil over them. Water runs everywhere, giving the faces voices. They recite spells, and the forest is filled with whisperings.

Looking at the landscape, you can easily let it all merge into one great blur of green. There are over 75 kinds, or species, of moss in the Bella Coola Valley, 35 kinds of lichens, 15 kinds of ferns and 425 kinds of flowering plants. It seems at first glance that the plants are growing in chaos together, the way voices mingle at a large gathering until the individual is lost and there is just babble. But in fact there is a pattern, a subtle, intricate zoning code, in which the plant species are separated and yet woven together, as threads in a tapestry.

At the estuary, along the edge of a grove of towering old-growth Sitka spruce, are ranks of cottonwood, alder, mountain ash and a few Pacific crab apple trees. Salmonberry, thimbleberry, wild rose and other shrubs are found in the understorey. Carpeting the forest floor are mosses, lady fern, oak fern and western swordfern, along with delicate flowers like wild lily of the valley. Where water collects to form dark bogs, skunk cabbages cluster, horsetail erupts and goatsbeard gathers. Standing apart in the drier soils are western columbine and fireweed. Closer to the moister, western edge of a tide-flat meadow shore lupine, Indian rice root and pallid paintbrush emerge—each adding its own shade of green to the portrait.

The organization and diversity of plant (and animal) species is typical of coastal temperate rain forests, which are among the oldest and most productive of all ecosystems on Earth. Tropical rain forests may have more kinds of plants and animals in a given area, but they do not come close to coastal forests such as this one in the mass of living things. The most productive valley bottoms on the north Pacific coast contain as much as 2000 tonnes of plant and other organic matter per hectare—twenty times as much as in a tropical rain forest. Scientists are only now coming to realize the value and complexity of coastal forests. Unfortunately, in many places the knowledge comes too late; massive clear-cutting has already taken place. No one knows what has been lost with the logging of places such as Long Island in southeast Alaska, stripped shore to shore, or in the Escalante region on Vancouver Island, which was laid waste by a paroxysm of logging that swept away every tree or left it shattered on the ground. From what remains in the Bella Coola Valley, we can get some idea of what once was.

The Nuxalk (new-halk), the first people to inhabit the valley, called the month of January Sxlikt—or the time of the Angry Moon. On a bitterly cold evening it is easy to understand why. In the clear night air the moon seems to loom over the shoulders of the mountains, its pale lunar face frowning down on the landscape. Although it is generally mild in the valley, in January a

RIVER OF THE ANGRY MOON

prevailing warm westerly can unexpectedly and abruptly change to a frigid east wind known to the Nuxalk as Sps. It has been interpreted as an act of fury and was feared as the Wind That Sweeps Away Food.

Sps brings chilling temperatures at any time in the late fall or in the winter. It blows from the northeast over the snow-covered Interior Chilcotin Plateau, where it has frozen ranchers' trucks to the ground, and roars down through the Bella Coola Valley. With gusts of 60 kilometres an hour, trees bend, large branches are set in motion, power lines are broken and waterfalls freeze into pillars of solid ice. On a day when it is only $-10°C$, Sps can create a wind chill of $-27°C$ in moments, driving birds and animals into hiding. Some, such as bears and jumping mice, are hibernating inside safe dens, their heartbeats slowed. Others, such as wood frogs, beetles and butterfly larvae, have become frozen alive. They will thaw from this temporary death in the spring and transform from within. Such is the patience of nature.

Some days, during the time of the Angry Moon, it is just too cold to fish. I am standing upstream from where the Bella Coola River empties into the estuary. I am bundled in three layers of underclothes, a down parka and wool mitts, and my face is covered with a woollen scarf that collects moist breath and turns it into ice crystals. It is so cold I can feel the air pass down my throat and enter my lungs. The sun glances off the estuary for only twenty minutes today, when the rays shine obliquely down Tatsquan River Valley. I look up to the mountaintops, where the brightness of the snow stands in sharp contrast to the deep blue sky. Great veils of powder are arcing from the peaks, trailing off downwind.

I am here to observe the highest tide of the year. Today, January 20, the sun, the earth and the moon are aligned, exerting the greatest gravitational pull of the year. The earth will not noticeably yield to this cosmic beckoning—but the ocean will. Shortly after noon the tide will stand at 5.3 metres; then it will begin to ebb, draining the tidal marshes, peeling back off the flats to expose the glistening mud and dropping the wharves so low that the gangplanks to shore take on a severe angle. By 7:30 P.M. it will hit slack, having dropped 5 metres. It is a monumental occurrence, which ties the valley to the heavens, but it happens so quietly, so routinely, that few notice.

Snow covers the ground. There is a shell of ice extending one-third of the way across the river from each shore. Between the ice shelves small icebergs and islands of slush churn towards the estuary. Some pile up on gravel bars; others crash into them and spin off. Although the tide is high enough to slow the flow of the Bella Coola, the wind is so strong that it overcomes even the power of the moon, and the river drives on into the ocean. Boats retreat from the inlet when Sps is blowing, not because of the rough seas, but because the spray torn from wave tops freezes on the rigging, on the decks, on the door handles and bundles of nets. There have been cases where a tonne or more of ice accumulated, capsizing boats and turning their masts into glaciated sea anchors. There are families in the valley who shudder when Sps rises, for in the moaning wind they hear voices from the past. They hear the sounds of breaking ice and of the sea rising over the hulls of white ships.

As the tide falls the desolate, dark brown mud flats slowly emerge, here and there marked by yellow, dead vegetation, and in the distance, brilliant in contrast, a flock of swans forage. In the shallow water they paddle their broad, black feet rapidly against the soft mud to loosen the roots of bulrushes and other plants. When the water drops you can see the craters they have dug, and the birds will linger there, staining their faces as they pull out the roots, their breath as white as down.

The vegetation in the estuary has been flattened into a tangled mat by the beating of winter rains and the press of heavy snow. Come spring the blended carpet of muted yellows and browns will rise in a hundred tones of green. Closest to the ocean the common mare's tail and soft-stemmed bulrushes will unfurl; next come the creeping spike rush and ranks of Lyngby's sedge, which is so rich in protein that grizzly bears emerge from the forest to feed on it after hibernation. Farther up the shore are silverweed, wild clover and tufted hair grass, followed by rows of marsh pea vine and common red paintbrush. Finally, prolific growth of sweet gale and black twinberry marks the transition to forest, where thick ranks of Sitka spruce stand, combing sea mist from the wind.

Out on the flats the tide eventually falls to reveal huge, twisted wads of cedar and spruce roots. The trunks are cut flat across by saw blades. These great trees once grew upstream, along the riverbanks outside an area that has long been protected by parkland. After logging swept through, the current undercut the stumps—and they wallowed downstream until they came to rest here, like dark, unsettling tombstones.

Of all the months of the year, January is the hardest for a fly-fisher on the Bella Coola. The wind interferes with back casts; lines freeze, hands become numb, and it is impossible to get a fly line to lie flat on water that is a slurry of ice. But you are tempted to try, because the glaciers have stopped melting and the silt, ground from the mountains, is held in ice. Beneath the slush the river runs low and clear.

High on the surrounding mountains the snow is stacked in great steeples. The sun has just disappeared for the day behind

Mount Fougner, which towers above the estuary. I cheer myself by remembering that each day now the sun will climb higher in the sky and each day will be three minutes longer than the day before. I look forward to the time when the river ice will begin to melt. Ahead lie longer days, warmer days, and I know that within a few weeks the snow will be gone from the valley bottom and the snow line will start to climb the hillsides.

It was not always so. There have been times in the not-so-distant past when the summer sun could not melt all the winter snow. As recently as thirteen thousand years ago a huge sheet of ice and snow covered the entire Bella Coola Valley twelve months of the year. At its maximum, some fourteen thousand to fifteen thousand years ago, the ice sheet exceeded 2000 metres in thickness, covering all but the highest mountain peaks. Then the summer heat began to win the fight for the land; the glaciers began to melt, the coastal lands began to appear once again, as if from under a great, frozen tide—and the Bella Coola River began to carve its cradle. Soon after that the fish returned, led by the steelhead, which is believed to be the progenitor of all Pacific salmon. It runs higher in the watershed than any of the others—and it alone can survive spawning. It is now the rarest of all the salmon.

From primitive salmonidae present in the Pacific Ocean 40 million years ago evolved whitefish, grayling, char, salmon and trout. Prehistoric fish looking much like modern trout were invading rivers and lakes by 3.5 million years ago. Subsequent adaptation led to the eventual development of coho, sockeye, chinook, chum, pink, cutthroat and steelhead or rainbow trout. All can be found in the Bella Coola River system. Some are in the river during the month of the Angry Moon, holding in sheltered water and waiting to spawn. Others have already laid their eggs, which will hatch when the days grow longer, and their

RIVER OF THE ANGRY MOON

decomposing bodies can be found hanging in snags or littering the high-water mark.

One of the miracles of a river is the way in which the fish species have evolved to ensure maximum use of the watershed and minimal interaction with one another. If you swim in a salmon spawning river when the water is low and clear, you will see the different races of fish apparently mixing together as they dart away from your shadow. But after a moment they always separate, schooling and agreeing on invisible factors that divide and define them. Through the chaos of nature, then, we see these parallel lines of order running. The salmon species divide the waters among themselves so that all might flourish in their own niche, just as the plants find their own place in the entwined forest and in the mat of vegetation that lies trampled along the windswept estuary.

But the salmon species do more than just separate one from the other, as chum from pinks, or coho from chinook. There are also distinctions within each order. There are steelhead that come back in three distinctly timed runs. There are coho that only spawn in the lower river and seemingly identical coho that always run high up the system. This species differentiation becomes even more pronounced when you look beyond the fish at the insect life along the river. There are 27 kinds of mayflies, for example, 40 kinds of stoneflies and 275 kinds of moths. Why? Why so many differences in one valley?

The simple answer is that over the eons the living creatures have evolved to fit the most subtle patterns of the landscape. They have shaped themselves to the river and to the forest in response to factors that even the most brilliant scientists are still groping to understand. One thing is abundantly clear, however: this is the way of nature—and it works.

A "law" of ecology states that everything is connected to everything else. Clearly when such a fantastically intricate natural order is disrupted by industrial clear-cut logging, commercial overfishing or the introduction of alien species it must have a profound impact, the long-term implications of which cannot be known to us. If a stock of salmon is eradicated, for example, it takes with it the unique genetic coding that had made it perfect for its niche. Unable to see the future, we cannot know what genetic traits might be needed ahead to survive disease outbreaks, or global warming. In this light the decline of the steelhead in the Bella Coola River, and in most rivers from California to Alaska, is deeply disturbing, for we simply don't know what is being lost. All we know is that they are being swept away as if by Sps, leaving the spawning beds empty under the shadows of the ancient glaciers.

As I walk through the forest the cadence of my step is picked up by the fly rod in my hand. The tip bounces to the rhythm of my feet. I can barely hear the river. It is softened by winter but whispers like the forest. Water covers stone and, lifting up, leaves a shimmering of ice along the margins. Mist rises from patches of dark water. Standing still beside the river, my rod unused, for I cannot find anywhere to cast, I become invisible. It is as if I were meant to wait, for within minutes a wolf passes, its eyes searching the shoreline, its ears hearing the secrets of moving water. It has thick grey fur that ripples over its shoulders, white leggings, and it breathes out clouds of river mist. When it is gone, swallowed by the forest, I know I have been blessed. I have fallen from the mountain and landed on my feet in the river as gently as rain.

Walking through the Bella Coola Valley in January it is hard to believe it is a place of such environmental richness. From under the snow peek somber tones of brown, black and dark green. The river seems devoid of life, except for the drifts of ice that turn and twist in the current. Then, from the stormy forest canopy, a weak, high-pitched voice falls. *See-see-see*, it begins before being lost again in the sound of the moving trees. After a moment it comes again. Overhead, close to the base of a large branch, is a flock of golden-crowned kinglets. The tiny, olive-grey birds, each as light as a pair of sugar cubes, are almost invisible, except for the occasional flash of a bright yellow stripe along the crown. They are the smallest songbirds in Canada, and today, as they search the bark of a five-hundred-year-old Sitka spruce, they are singing in defiance of Sps. Soon the moon will change its face.

February

Moon When There Is Nothing

Early in February the sun finally rises above Nuxalk Mountain and the eastern edge of Mount Fougner as it completes its east-to-west arc across the sky. The change is dramatic because direct sunlight falling on the town of Bella Coola suddenly increases from minutes to almost four hours in one day. No doubt the early Nuxalk celebrated this moment with their hypnotic dancing that is as transfixing as a narcotic. Even today I notice a remarkable uplifting effect in the small community when it is first bathed in sunlight for most of the morning. People look up, holding out their arms to catch the light. It is as if the weight of winter has suddenly lifted off the land. Yet the weather can still bring violent, cold storms this month, for the seasons are on the edge of transition.

The Nuxalk called the second moon after winter solstice Atoansdimut, or Moon When There Is Nothing. And the reason seems clear enough. No new runs of fish enter the river this month. Plants have yet to push out the first green tendrils of spring. Many hibernating animals, such as the grizzly bear, alligator lizard, marmot, western toad, garter snake and western jumping mouse, remain hidden in their dens in a suspended state. Other animals, such as the pika, wood rat, chipmunk and squirrel, spend days huddled in a torpor, although they don't hibernate. When the weather warms, they awaken to feed on their food caches, leaving their tracks patterned through the snow, but then return to their dens to sleep. This is a time of waiting for life to begin again.

In the estuary the commercial fishing boats lie empty at the docks, crusted in ice. The weather is too cold to do much, so the fishers are content cutting wood and keeping the home fires going. The cattle, penned since November, are eating hay in their lowland corrals; like the ranchers, they are expending a minimum of effort. But a few people are busy. The loggers started back to work this week, falling and hauling the forest to faraway coastal mills, where workers are busy cutting the timber into boards or mulching it into toilet paper.

For a fly-fisher, the warmer days of February provide the first opportunities to really be out on the water again. It's a good time to try for mountain whitefish, a small, obscure fish that most sports anglers ignore. In the past, fishers had more choice at this time of year. Up until the early 1970s, anglers could fish for chinook just off the dock and hook up to twelve a day. Or they could try for 3- to 9-kilogram winter steelhead in the Bella Coola, especially in the deeper pools around Firvale. It was nothing, they say, to catch six in a day. In the 1980s, you could fly-fish for sea-run cutthroat in the pools of the lower river and catch up to eighty a day. But the history of each of these remarkable fisheries is similar: there would be fantastic catches initially, followed by steady decline and, finally, almost no fish.

Despite such problems, mountain whitefish, a distant relative of the salmon, are still in the river in good number. Whitefish are troutlike in shape, with backs that range from light brown to olive-green. They have small, soft mouths, which lack teeth, and noticeably large cycloid scales—features that distinguish them from salmon and trout.

The average length is 20 to 30 centimetres, but they often get up to 45 centimetres and 1.5 kilograms. The largest mountain whitefish on record was 4 pounds, 7 ounces (about 2 kilograms), 22.5 inches (57 centimetres) long, and was caught in the Lardeau River, in Canada's Northwest Territories. Some of the whitefish in the Bella Coola system are in that range. Fisheries workers who net the Atnarko for salmon brood stock say they have seen whitefish that could set a new world record.

The larger, more mature whitefish appear to vacate the pools of the Atnarko after fall spawning. They move down to the Bella Coola River to pools around Steep Roof, where they will spend the winter in deep water. In February and March, as the water warms and sunlight increases, they begin to migrate back to the Atnarko.

It is something of a miracle that they are even here, for whitefish spend their entire lives in fresh water and have no tolerance for salt water. To reach the Bella Coola system it would have been impossible for whitefish to come up the coast, following the retreating glaciers, as the salmon did. When the thick polar ice cap covering much of North America (including the northern third of the Columbia River system) began to melt, a series of large glacial lakes formed in its wake. Mountain whitefish spread to the inland of British Columbia from the Columbia River system by invading the glacial lakes and streams that flowed from them. Their path can be traced first through the glacial lakes in the Okanagan Valley, then through those in the

Shuswap Valley and on to the Fraser River through central British Columbia. Eventually they made their way up the Chilcotin River and into the Atnarko. In those early days, Charlotte Lake and the upper Atnarko River flowed east to the Fraser River system. When the Bella Coola system eventually captured the upper reaches of the Atnarko, the whitefish were shifted west. What a huge, calamitous place the world was then, with massive glaciers covering what is now rich forest or ranch land. The rivers must have been gargantuan, brawling torrents in flood. But in the winter they would have calmed, as the Bella Coola does now. The sediment load would have dropped, and the fish would have come nosing upstream, pushing as far as they could go.

Whitefish were not the only species to come "overland." Longnose sucker, redside shiner, coarse scale sucker and northern squawfish came by the same route. In pioneer days there was also a large char, well known to the early white settlers on the Atnarko, which was undoubtedly a bull trout, another saltwater-intolerant fish that originated in the Columbia River.

Early white settlers used to call the bull trout Lonesome Lake Dollies, thinking they were large Dolly Varden, a char named after a Charles Dickens character who sported a brightly coloured petticoat. Bull trout are a recently recognized species of char. They are larger and broader and have a proportionately larger head than Dolly Varden. According to the International Game Fish Association, any char other than lake trout or brook trout weighing over 12 pounds (5.5 kilograms) taken in the bull trout/Dolly Varden range is probably a bull trout.

The late Isabel Edwards, a pioneer who spent her last days in Bella Coola Hospital, sometimes told stories of catching Dollies the size of salmon. She measured some and found they were up to 90 centimetres long and 45 centimetres thick.

"We caught them on pieces of mouse flesh, or red kinnikinnick berries, that would work as good sometimes," she said, her eyes full of delight as she recalled dropping a line into the dark water, all those years ago. "It didn't take a lot of skill, and pretty soon you'd have enough for a meal."

Isabel, who had a tough, independent spirit until the end, at age eighty-six, fished from a raft, anchored by a rock at the end of a long rope. She caught most of her giant fish in the early 1930s, in a deep hole of the Atnarko River, just across from a cabin built by a neighbouring trapper, Frank Ratcliff. The well-built cabin is still there, its wood bleached by age, but the pool is gone, covered by the shallow waters of Stillwater Lake, which was created in 1936. When a flash flood roared down Goat Creek, tonnes of rocks spilled across the Atnarko, making a natural dam that caused the river to back up. By the time a new channel was cut, the water had spread out above, forming the lake that now laps at the door of the old Ratcliff place. Isabel's pool is still down there somewhere, under the surface. Perhaps if you found it and drifted a hook into the shadows, baited with a mouse, there might come an urgent tug from the netherworld.

Old-timers in the valley, such as Elijah Gurr, talk about casting half a muskrat impaled on a large halibut hook into Lonesome Lake, a narrow, windswept body of water in the mountains above the Bella Coola Valley. They would leave it out overnight and then drag in a monster Dolly in the morning. According to the stories, the fish got up to 35 pounds (16 kilograms). The biggest Bella Coola bull trout I ever saw a picture of was caught by Lloyd Brynildsen near McCall Flats in 1955. It was 37 inches (94 centimetres) long, 18 inches (46 centimetres) in girth, and weighed 16 pounds, 14 ounces (about 7.6 kilograms). It won the prize for the largest Dolly Varden in the 1955 Hunting and

RIVER OF THE ANGRY MOON

Fishing Championship in North America. Lloyd won a fishing reel. The amazing thing is, he lost an even bigger fish. Here's the story he tells:

"The day before I had been fishing there just below a log-jam. Something took my lure. It swam upstream and I couldn't stop it. It just swam upriver, slowly swam away. Not violent. Nothing I could do, I just kept snubbing up, snubbing up, and then the line broke. It just swam away. I had about 20-pound test. It was a heavy fish. The next day something—another big fish—bit my lure and then slowly swam away. But this fish swam downstream, swam down a little bit. Not fast, at his own pace. Shaking its head once in a while, but not a violent fight. I eventually got it near shore, got alongside him and got a look at the fish. The side flippers were white edged and about five inches long! The fish had a face on it like a lingcod. An ugly fish! It had a whole cutthroat in its belly."

No one seems to have caught a bull trout in the Bella Coola River system for many years now. Most people believe they are extinct. If they are, it is a case of a slow-growing, long-lived, low-reproducing species running out of niche space. Overfishing will do that. Still, the Bella Coola is a large system and maybe there are a few rare bull trout lurking under logjams, in Isabel's drowned pool or in the depths of Lonesome Lake, fish as big as the one that attacked Lloyd Brynildsen's bait and slowly stretched his line until it snapped.

By contrast to the bull trout, whitefish are small, almost fairylike creatures. On a February day, with a gentle breeze blowing from the east, I set out to find some. On the drive to Fisheries Pool, a well-known campsite on the Atnarko near the small community of Stuie, I watch for snowshoe hare, mule deer and Columbia blacktail, which sometimes appear along the road, even in the month of nothing. And if they are about, there's a chance you may catch a rare glimpse of a cougar or wolf, or at least see the trails they have left in the snow, hunting from cover to cover.

Earlier I had crossed the tracks of a wolf in a fresh fall of snow. I followed it along the forest edge, through the trees, heading towards the river. The footprints ran to a place where the frozen bodies of coho salmon lay on a gravel bar. I could see where the wolf had clawed at a fish and chewed on its skin.

The weather changes in the short time it takes to drive up the valley from Bella Coola. The wind is beginning to blow in gusts—raising debris from the roadside and making the small trees sway. The rattle of branches fills the air, as if a great Native dance is about to begin. The clouds are high; the air temperature has warmed slightly to minus $-1\,^\circ$C. A light snow is falling, but the wind drives it from the road before it has a chance to collect.

The trail leads through a forest of large, majestic Douglas firs. Under the pale February sun the snow pack has softened. Each step now breaks through the crust into knee-deep drifts. I am hot by the time I reach the river and a little out of breath. An ice sheet extends a metre or so from shore, giving the dark water a stark edge. Small icicles glisten and drip from branches near the water. The river is low, clear and the same temperature as the air.

Upstream a splash reveals a pair of spawned-out coho, still bonded even in the last moments of their lives. Not long ago the salmon were thick bodied and bright silver, with dark black spots splattered over their green backs. Now they are pale, shrunken by a third since entering the river, and they show the scars of spawning—frayed fins, gaping wounds, fungal infection, blindness. Side by side, they are barely holding their position in the water. The female turns upside down and struggles to keep from drifting away. Soon, perhaps in hours, both will be dead. The emotion this realization stirs in me is not sadness but reverence. It is a natural event, part of the process in which the nutrients from the sea are returned to the river.

On the other side of the pool, sitting among the snow-covered branches of a large black cottonwood, an almost perfectly camouflaged bald eagle patiently waits. It is a stunning sight, and without the salmon it would not be here. Nor would a solitary, sooty-grey, wrenlike bird perching on a large boulder. It begins to sing a clear, sweet, burbling series of trills and flute-like whistles. If it were not for its lovely call, you might not notice the bird, because its colours blend so well with the blue-grey waters and wet stones. It is a dipper, a common resident of western streams. About the size of a starling, it is a chunky bird with short wings, a short tail and a slender, straight, laterally compressed bill. In summer, dippers can be seen along fast-flowing riffles of coastal streams from sea level to the highest alpine meadows. In late fall, snow and ice force dippers to the valley bottom where they stay until spring, returning to the headwaters to build small nests among the stones. They lay three or four tiny white eggs.

Dippers boldly dive into fast currents where no fly-fisher would dare to wade. And they are well equipped for cold water, with a warm, thick undercoat of down. Water is kept out of their nostrils by protective skin flaps and out of their eyes by a third eyelid. Strong, short wings enable dippers to swim to the bottom of deep pools, where they run along the rocks, collecting insects or drifting fish eggs. Sometimes one will dart from a perch to try for a dry fly.

The dipper's behaviour is a beautiful adaptation to its habitat of cold, clear, rushing water. For a few minutes it anxiously bobs up and down, dipping; then it hops off its rocky perch into the water. After a few seconds it pops back up with a bright orange, pearl-shaped coho egg in its beak. It swallows its prize and dives again. This time it surfaces with a small fish, which it proudly deposits on the snowy riverbank. As I approach, the bird lets out a loud, sharp call note, *dzeet*, and takes off in a blur of grey, flying downstream in a swift, straight line just above the water surface. The fish in the snow is a juvenile coho. Beautifully coloured, the upper half of the body is gold, with a row of oval spots of dark brown pigment known as parr marks. The fins are tinged with orange, which seems a remarkable colour for camouflage. The coho is still alive, so I slip it into the water, where it quickly swims out of sight. Perhaps one day it will return here to spawn.

At Fisheries Pool the air vibrates as slides of snow and rock cascade down steep slopes. Across the river to the southwest is a series of spectacular granite peaks surrounding logged-out Tsini Tsini Valley. To the east is Mount Melikan, and to the west Mount Stupendous. The blue-grey granitic cliffs are highlighted by snow on the talus slopes.

The Nuxalk word for the river here is *Stwic*, which means "place to rest," and it's peaceful as I look through the reflected surface to the stone bed of the river. Under the smooth, gliding water are the myriad colours of the gravels. There are salt-and-pepper granitic rocks and an array of other subtle colours, ranging from burnt orange to dark brown, purple, grey, green and white. These are fragments from the mountains collected, polished and settled on the bottom by the river over thousands of years. Some of the stones are volcanic; the grey rock comes from a lava flow millions of years old.

The orange to dark brown gravel, which is reflected in the colouration of coho fry, is basaltic rock that originally came from three large shield volcanoes. The Rainbow Range, so-called because of its brightly stained slopes, is all that remains of them. They were active 6 to 8 million years ago.

The purple and fine-grained greenish rocks, some of which contain large white flecks or crystals, came from ancient volcanoes that were active over 135 million years ago. Erosion long ago removed all remnants of the volcanic mountains, but the pieces lie here at my feet, mixed with greenstone, a form of metamorphic rock extruded onto the earth's surface 180 million years ago as basalt and andesite. It is the most common rock in the Bella Coola Valley.

Before I begin casting I stir the gravel with my foot and uncover a variety of aquatic insect nymphs and larvae. I have found the sequestered activity of February. In fact, this is the most active time of year for aquatic insects. Many of the larvae and nymphs are now almost fully grown, so they are easily seen, collected and identified.

The gravel is a precious part of the river ecosystem. It provides shelter for fish eggs and is the protected nursery for emergent salmon. Sometimes in the gravel you'll uncover small creatures that look like black eels. They are immature lamprey known as Ammocetes larvae—descendants of ostracoderms, which inhabited the oceans over 400 million years ago. Also sheltered in the gravel are mayflies, caddis flies, stoneflies and a group known as dipterans, which includes chironomids, no-see-ums, black flies, mosquitoes and crane flies, all of which are prime food for salmonids.

It is no coincidence that the Atnarko River has the greatest number and variety of aquatic insects in the Bella Coola River system *and* the greatest biomass of salmon and trout. Research has shown that streams such as the Atnarko can produce as much as

115 to 225 kilograms of nymphs and larvae per hectare of gravel bottom. It is this rich web of life that supports the salmon and trout during their early years.

Fish feed on insects wherever they can find them. Some aquatic insects are simply picked up off the bottom. Others are intercepted after they release their grip on rocks so that the current will carry them to a new location, in what is known to fishermen as "the drift." During a drift, trout will suddenly become more active and anglers will say that "the bite is on." It can go off again just as quickly.

Most aquatic insects emerge from coastal streams during April, May and June. But early in the year, before the snow has melted, many aquatic insects have already started hatching. On warm days in February and early March, I watch for the little blue-wing olive, the snow sedge and the tiny winter black stoneflies.

I know that in February Atnarko whitefish will be feeding on some of the clingers, insects that use their claws to hold onto stones. Walking upstream through the shallows, I search the deeper waters. And finally I see it—a flash of burnt gold in the depths, signalling foraging whitefish.

Mountain whitefish like to feed on insect larvae in the gravel. With their relatively small mouths, they can suck food from between the stones. In an effort to maintain a head-down position for feeding, whitefish rotate in the water, with each twist sending a flash of light off their sides.

I walk upstream about 18 metres from the grubbing white-fish before carefully wading into the water. I select a size 14 hare's ear, a tiny thatch of fur and feather, because it crudely resembles so many small, dark brown aquatic nymphs. Facing downstream slightly I begin to cast, unfurling the line over the reflective surface. The first cast is mended quickly, throwing a loop upstream, to allow the fly to drift deep. Any touch on the line now will signal a fish has mouthed the fly. Nothing. The second cast goes upstream about 40 degrees, to give the fly more time to sink. Just as the line straightens below me, I feel the fly ticking on the river bottom. This is where I want it to be. I cast again, allowing the fly to drift freely. There it is, a gentle bump, an almost imperceptible resistance on the line. I lift the rod and feel the fish, throbbing in the dark water. It sends out a flurry of golden flashes. After a short, gamy fight I bring it onto the snow-bank. It's a big fish of a kilogram or more with bright silver sides and a belly as white as dipper eggs.

Whitefish stocks are among the healthiest in the river. If I kill one or two each year, I won't harm the population. But I could take twenty-five whitefish, according to the fisheries regulations. I could give my catch away, or throw it into the garden, and come back and do the same tomorrow.

Fisheries managers argue that generous catch limits are justified because the whitefish population is so healthy. That logic might apply to a marketplace, where an abundance of stock means there is a surplus. (And, as any sales clerk knows, the surplus must go.) But nature is not a dry goods store. If abundance is seen for what it really is—a sign that the stocks are in perfect balance—then regulations should be set conservatively to ensure that the population does not decline.

It is unlikely that whitefish will ever become a popular sports fish in the Bella Coola River. Mostly they are too small. But skilled anglers could start hunting for the bigger specimens, perhaps hoping for a new world record. If that ever happens, it may only be a matter of time before mountain whitefish populations begin to fall—like the steelhead, cutthroat, bull trout and coho before them.

Fishing slowly down through the pool, I hook four more fat whitefish, killing a second to make a brace and letting the others go. Darkness falls early, and going up through the snowy woods, the fish gently bumping against my waders, I feel as if I have performed magic—conjuring a harvest from the Moon of Nothing.

March

~

Moon of the
Herring Spawn

To the Nuxalk, March brings the Moon of the Herring Spawn, when the silver fish swarm in from the sea to shower their eggs like glittering pollen on a forest of seaweed. It is also when the eulachon return, a writhing upstream current of blue-backed smelt that floods into the river with the tide, setting the dogs barking and causing men to run from their homes with nets. And as spring begins to unfold, chum salmon emerge from their gravel nests by the millions, their tender, translucent bodies drawn from the darkness of the riverbed by the soft light above.

March is a time of movement and energy, when life can be felt surging back into the valley, and it might be called the Moon of Small Fishes. The herring start it all, and their spawning was once the dominant natural event of early spring. Along the Pacific coast, from California to Alaska, herring mass in great schools for a few weeks each year as they seek sheltered bays in which to lay their eggs on fronds of brown kelp, stalks of green sea grass and other brightly coloured plants that have skins as rough as toads or as slick as eels. The spawning progresses from south to north up along the continental edge. At the southern end of the range, down around Monterey and San Francisco Bay, it starts in November—at the northern end, up past Ketchikan and on to Auke Bay, the runs come as late as July. On the central coast, in North Bentinck Arm, the herring arrive just as the ice melts on the Bella Coola's side streams and as the migratory birds begin to return.

Winter fishing for chinook was memorable off Bella Coola when the salmon, known locally as "feeder springs," crowded into the estuary following schools of herring. The glistening, silver baitfish often milled about under the docks in great, green-backed shoals for weeks before the spawn began.

"The whole bay, from Talheo Cannery to Clayton Falls, was alive with sea gulls and many species of diving ducks along with harbor seals and sea lions," recalls Al Purkiss, a retired commercial fisherman and long-time resident of the valley. "To the anglers, it was a great delight, for one never knew what to expect. The springs were the prize, but there always was the other good fare too—soles, flounders, halibut, gray cod and even black cod.

"One winter I believe there were two hundred salmon caught by the Buzz Bombers off the old dock."

That year people stood on the wharves or cast from the decks of moored boats, probing the dark waters with Buzz Bombs, simple metal lures that spiralled and spun like dying herring, drawing attacks from all kinds of fish.

Purkiss remembers that about 1980 the herring just stopped coming and the estuary fell silent. Soon the fish-eating birds were gone, the schools of black cod, dogfish, sole and salmon drifted away. You could cast a Buzz Bomb for hours, feeling the lifeless thud of the lure's weight as it tugged against your line and peering down into the water off the end of the dock without seeing a single herring glint.

"Perhaps there are no more salmon around to herd the winter herring back up the inlets anymore," he muses.

When the chinook were in, Purkiss used to be able to go out in a small rowboat and cast hooks baited with fresh herring, taking his limit in an hour or two. The fish seemed to be waiting. One angler told of a 5.5-kilogram chinook that grabbed his spoon just as it hit the water, in a strike so sudden and violent the fish must have watched the lure falling from the sky.

One season several fin-clipped salmon were caught. The anglers turned in the heads and later learned the chinook were Columbia River hatchery stock that had been feeding near the northern limit of their oceanic range.

Chinook salmon have disappeared from ninety-five streams in the Columbia River basin. Other Columbia salmon are also in danger. Sixty-five salmon stocks have become extinct, and 143 of the remaining 200 are in decline. The story of the Columbia River is one of the great tragedies of salmon management. At one time 16 million salmon returned each year to the Columbia. Then the river was dammed, spawning grounds were flooded, and migration routes were blocked. Now only 2.5 million salmon return, and the loss is still felt far to the north, in Bella Coola, and up the coast into Alaska. But the question unanswered in North Bentinck arm is, did the herring vanish first, or the Columbia springs?

Herring roe, or *kazunoko,* is a delicacy in Japan, where it sells for up to $300 a pound—a huge markup from the $20 paid to fishers in North America. But even at that low price, on the British Columbia coast, where the harvest is measured in thousands of tons, the value of roe drives a frantic fishery that has wiped out stocks in some areas. Herring no longer spawn on the beaches in the estuary at Bella Coola, for example, but are found farther down the inlet, indicating either a localized extinction or a dramatic shift in behaviour. Overall the North Pacific herring population is considered healthy, but stocks are less than half historical levels. Heavy fishing combined with naturally weak runs devastated the fishery in the mid-60s, leading to a four-year ban on harvesting herring. Since then, stocks have slowly been rebuilt, but in some areas the herring have never returned. There are many bays and channels all along the coast where the herring no longer spawn. For those places it is as if a piece of spring itself has been lost.

About 510 million herring spawn annually in the central coast area of British Columbia; an estimated 24 million of them in North Bentinck Arm, far removed from the estuary. When they spawn, the water along the shore turns white with a tide of milt.

The Nuxalk have long used herring for food, catching the fish in dip nets or in fish traps along the estuary, or collecting the long fronds of kelp where the tiny, clear eggs stick in thick clusters. They also found that herring eggs could be gathered by setting fir or hemlock branches in the frothy water. The fish conveniently draped the branches with their eggs, like fruit, and the Nuxalk had only to pull the heavy, dripping branches back to shore to have the makings of a feast.

Commercial fisheries are supposed to take no more than 20 per cent of returning herring, but overfishing is commonplace, with fleets often hauling in thousands of tonnes in excess of their targets. Many argue that the commercial fishery should be greatly restricted so that more herring will be available for the fish and other animals that depend on them. Chinook and coho, two salmon stocks that are in decline, have a diet that is about 60 per cent herring. And studies from the Gulf of Alaska suggest that sea lions, seabirds and other predators are going hungry. The populations of many species are dropping. Scientists don't know why this is happening. The commercial overfishing of herring, squid, cod and pollock may be to blame, however. The impact of a krill fishery in British Columbia, which began in the 1990s, is unknown. But it could prove disastrous, for krill are a fundamental link in the food web—feeding the herring that feed the salmon.

While herring no longer spawn in the Bella Coola estuary, the eulachon still arrive, drawing with them a flurry of life. Before the eulachon spawn, you can sense the energy level rising around Bella Coola. It's not just the activity around the docks, where herring skiffs are being made ready—it's in the air too. You sense it in the way the birds stir in the estuary. Milling about are gulls, ravens, crows, great blue herons, bald eagles, murrelets, grebes, goldeneyes, common mergansers, scaups and buffleheads. All are waiting for the feast to begin—the feast to end winter.

The birds send the first signal that the smelt have arrived. Wheeling up in white clouds above the flats and filling the air with their cries are thousands of mew, ringed, herring, glaucous-winged, California and Bonaparte's gulls. They spin and dive and dance on the water, plucking fish with each drop of their head. They are joined by flocks of more than twenty kinds of birds, and soon the air is wild with their calls. In the background is a deep, guttural roar—sea lions pressing in on the smelt schools from the ocean side. The sound echoes over the forest and wakes the dogs in the village. Soon word has spread and people can be seen piling nets into their pickup trucks and racing to the estuary. Drifting downstream in a kayak, I peer into the clear river and see dark clouds flaring away from my shadow, which is rippling across the bottom. It is a school of eulachon, and after a moment it turns and races up underneath me. As they pass the surface stirs, and along the shoreline some fish are forced onto the gravel, where they jump and twist, sparkling on the stones. It crosses my mind that these fish might take a tiny fly drifted among them, but there seems little point. Beaching on a rocky bar I take a net and dip out a handful of vibrating, electric-blue fish, which are about 20 to 25 centimetres long. It's as easy as that.

For thousands of years the Nuxalk have harvested the eulachon—the fish of fire—rendering them into a rich golden oil in cedar chests known as stink boxes that are set up at fishing sites along the river. When Alexander Mackenzie traipsed through here in 1793, becoming the first European to reach the west coast of North America overland, he did it by following a well-beaten grease trail that led through the mountains from the Interior. The trail got its name from the eulachon oil that was spilled, leaving dark stains on the earth, as Native traders made the trek up through the Coast Mountains, carrying the oil in boxes on their backs. At times the Nuxalk stored oil in the dried bulbs of kelp. They mixed it with most of their foods and used it as a preservative and a medicine. When settlers first arrived they discovered that dried eulachon were so rich in oil they would burn like candles—light from the sea, spitting and crackling in the darkness. Today eulachon populations are in wide decline. No one knows why, but ocean trawl fisheries, which take them by accident, and logging on coastal streams, which leads to siltation of spawning beds, are likely culprits. Today the Nuxalk harvest about 150,000 fish each March. It would be culturally devastating for the Native people to lose this fishery, yet because it is not commercially significant, little is being done to save the eulachon.

In the river at about this time a very different event is taking place, one that is not celebrated by the Native people, but that is just as important in nature—and to anglers. The chum fry are emerging from their stone nurseries—and the Dolly Varden are gathering to meet them.

Dolly Varden resemble trout in size and shape, but they are easily distinguished by the orange or red spots splattered along their flanks. Their backs are olive-green with deep green wavy markings, and the pectoral, pelvic and anal fins have a pinkish-white border. They are stunning fish.

Sea-run Dolly Varden fresh from the ocean are pale silver, as if the salt has absorbed the brightness of their colours. But the vibrant reds and oranges soon flare back to life, and when they get ripe for spawning, later in the year, they develop fire-orange bellies and scarlet fins.

At sea, anadromous Dolly Varden eat mainly herring, capelin, sand lance and crustaceans (shrimp and crab larvae), polychaete worms and salmon fry. When they come back into fresh water they feed on aquatic insects and salmon eggs found drifting along the gravel bottom. Few of the salmon eggs eaten would have hatched, because they had fallen outside the nest. Sea-run Dolly Varden wintering in lakes feed on aquatic insects, isopods, freshwater clam larvae and other bottom organisms. They also eat leeches and sockeye salmon fry.

In the spring Dolly Varden are voracious feeders. They will take a dry fly, but a salmon fry imitation is what they really want. If you fish a small streamer just under the surface, a Dolly will often come up to engulf it in a languid rise, rolling over it with a sideways turn of the head or taking it straight on, with first the head appearing and then the tail in what is called a porpoise rise. Sometimes they will be in a hurry and will come up so fast that they jump clear of the water to take the fly. In March, the fish are firm and lean; by summer they will have softened and grown fat.

Many people believe sea-run Dolly Varden are a threat to salmon, and sometimes along the river bank you'll find a fish amid the rocks, its colours faded, its skin drawn tight in the air, its neck broken. In an effort to cull unwanted predators, sports anglers often kill Dolly Varden and throw them away. The mentality is rooted in a time when predator control was a management tool. In the early 1900s sea-run Dolly Varden were singled out as being the most serious predator of salmon young and eggs. This condemnation was based on the finding that during the spring anglers caught char that were stuffed full of salmon fry. The truth is that almost all predators, from fish to birds and otters and snakes, gorge themselves when the fry emerge. Dolly Varden were no worse than any other, but that didn't stop Alaska Fish and Game managers from instituting a large-scale bounty program. Over 6 million char were destroyed, and more than $300,000 was spent between 1921 and 1940, when the program was finally abandoned.

The future of sea-run Dolly Varden is uncertain. Their slow growth and complex biology make them a fragile resource. Stocks are rapidly disappearing from streams along the Pacific coast because of overfishing and habitat destruction. On the central coast of British Columbia, thirty-six out of forty watersheds that produce sea-run trout have already been logged. Almost all were clear-cut.

On the Bella Coola the days when one could see hundreds of sea-run Dolly Varden feeding frantically on salmon fry in the deep pools are gone. But there are still pockets of char to be found, particularly in the spring, when the fry are emerging.

Responding to a signal that to me is as strong as the call that brings the birds to the inlet for the herring spawn, I gather my tackle early in March and set out to find the Dolly Varden, dressed in all their finery. Little Snootli Run is located near Walker Island Park, just a few kilometres up the valley from the Bella Coola townsite. A winding forest trail leads to an old channel of the Bella Coola River. Following the path under dripping cedars, I come to a shallow, glassy run where Snootli Creek merges with the larger river. You know right away you are looking at a fishing place. There are no trout rising or jumping, but the way the currents meld, the way the clean water slips around the rocks and laps at the shore, sets your senses on edge.

This place was once the site of a village known as Snutl, which means Home of the Big Dog Salmon. At one time a forest of giant fir, Sitka spruce and red cedar grew here. Although remnants of this forest can still be found on both sides of the river, most of the area has been cleared. In its place grows a forest of immature western hemlock, red cedar, cottonwood, alder and maple. Under the dark forest is a thick layer of willows, red elderberry, gooseberry, currant, salmonberry and thimbleberry, with branches that are shades of red, brown and yellow. The naked canes rattle when you brush them, and fine, shining raindrops cascade onto your shoulders. In a week or two silver pussy willows will emerge, and then the leaves will begin to tenderly unfurl.

Few plants are brave enough to begin to grow this early in March, but as I walk the path I catch a faint but unmistakably pungent odour. Somewhere nearby are the brilliant yellow spathes of the skunk cabbage, blooming amid the black muck they take root in. Once the spathe is fully grown, it will unfold to reveal a thick stalk bearing hundreds of small, greenish-yellow flowers. Later the large, fleshy oval leaves will burst forth. The leaves can grow to be 140 centimetres long and 74 centimetres wide—vegetation so enormous you would expect to encounter it in a tropical rain forest. The plant is named after the sour but somehow fragrant scent it emits. Like the other strong-smelling flowers of the valley—the chocolate lily and the mountain ash —the odour is designed to attract pollinating flies and beetles. I have come to think of it as the smell of spring, the smell of fishing.

Some coastal Indian tribes ate the boiled young leaves of the skunk cabbage as a vegetable, while others roasted the root in pits and even steamed the flower stalks. But the plant is said to have an acrid taste (due to calcium oxalate crystals), and some authorities classify it as poisonous. Whatever the skunk cabbage is like, grizzly bears love it and seek it out shortly after emerging from their winter dens. Once when I was fishing I saw great chunks of skunk cabbage leaves floating down the river. I waded noisily upstream and found a muddy patch where plants had been uprooted, as if someone had used a shovel to turn them over. There were tracks along the river bank, toes splayed by ponderous weight, the claws cleaving sharp lines in the earth as the great, padded feet lifted up. The bear was close somewhere, his forelegs and face stained with dark mud, his breath acrid. I tried to catch the musty scent of him, but all I could smell was the yellow fragrance of the skunk cabbages. I went back to the river and waded deep, the current pushing long strides out of me.

At the mouth of the Snootli River, I take my bearings. There is a gentle breeze blowing from the east. Patches of illuminated light and fragments of blue sky can be seen through the patterned cloud deck. A few of the mountaintops are covered with rounded stratocumulus clouds. The water of the nearby Bella

RIVER OF THE ANGRY MOON

Coola River is so clear I can see sand grains stirred by the current and flecks of minerals in the rocks.

I see a snow sedge sitting motionless on the bud of a willow shrub. Its wings are reddish-brown, with a long silver streak down the centre. A little blue-winged olive mayfly flutters past, seemingly out of control, as it heads in the direction of the blowing wind. Hiding among the crevices of rocks at my feet are black stoneflies with dark, smoky wings. The flight of these small stoneflies is fascinating to watch, for it provides insight into how insect flight may have evolved 350 million years ago. Winter stoneflies are an ancient group of insects. Rather than emerge from nymphal skins and fly up and away into the sky, as most aquatic insects do, winter stoneflies simply skim across the water to shore, where they hide among rocks. They are like tiny Everglades airboats as they race across the surface. Scientists believe this behaviour marks a transition in the development of flight— evolution's next step was to get airborne, but the stonefly dates from a time when wings did not equal flight.

The most common aquatic insects are tiny black chironomids, two-winged insects that look like little mosquitoes but that cannot bite. They are seen year-round, sometimes dancing in huge mating swarms, and are an important source of food for fish, particularly in the larval stage. Chironomids are arguably the most common aquatic insect in British Columbia's coastal freshwater streams, lakes and ponds. In some streams, the larvae of chironomids comprise up to 80 per cent of the total insect population of the stream.

On a nearby salmonberry bush a chickadee is busy tearing apart a gall, a small blister of bark that has formed on one of the canes. In a thicket that grows along Snootli Creek there are dozens of similar galls, some of them up to 7.5 centimetres in length and more than a centimetre in diameter. The little chickadee has discovered a rich source of food, for inside the blisters are small white grubs, which have built shelters for the winter. There are many kinds of galls on many kinds of plants. Mites, plant lice, flies, bees and moths all build galls. Nobody seems to know exactly how the insect makes the plant tissue grow into the bulbous shape, but some people can tell which insect is responsible by the way the gall looks and by the kind of plant it's on. The insect that hatches from the salmonberry galls looks like an ant with wings.

The chickadee is not alone as it works its way through the forest understorey. There are birds all around me. Most are hidden in the green wetness of the dark forest, but I can hear them singing, their melodious notes ringing out in a valley that was so recently silent, except for the sound of the wind. I can hear the happy *chick-a-dee-dee-dee* of the black-capped chickadee and the harsher *chick-a-chickadee* of the chestnut-backed chickadee. In the distance is the simple trill of the dark-eyed junco and the loud, raucous *shack-shack-shack* of the Steller's jay, a bird that always seems to be scolding. Echoing somewhere in the background is the low, guttural *krock* of the raven, a sound that perhaps more than any other captures the mystery of the forest.

More subtle is the distinctive "drumming" of the red-breasted sapsucker, which consists of several rapid taps followed by a short pause and then a series of slower, more rhythmic taps. This is the drumbeat of spring. I move deeper into the woods to try to catch a glimpse of this shy bird. I hear its weak, nasal call, *keerr*, look up, and there on the sun-exposed trunk of a large, rotting birch snag is a stunning bird. Its head, throat and upper breast are a deep, almost gaudy crimson; the rest of the upper parts are black and finely mottled with white. After a minute it goes back to lapping up sweet sap that is oozing out of parallel rows of square holes—holes that it drilled a few days before and that it has revisited now that they're filled with sap and insects. The bird holds its beak close to the hole, sucking up the sap; then throws back its head and swigs it down. Although sap-suckers are listed as being resident in coastal valleys, they leave Bella Coola Valley by October to winter in more southerly regions, such as Vancouver Island. Their return, in early March, is important to many animals, for squirrels, warblers and others feed at the sap wells. For decades, bird-watchers marvelled as tiny hummingbirds returned to Canada in early spring, often arriving before the blooming of the flowers they depended on for nectar. The birds were out of synch with their main source of food, and yet the indefatigable migrators pressed on, posing a puzzle that intrigued biologists for years. It is now believed the rufous hummingbird is influenced more by the range of sap-suckers than by the distribution of flowers. Sap is very similar to flower nectar, and hummingbirds will use sapsucker trees to sustain themselves until the flowers bloom. The sugar-rich sap flowing from trees is also used by the early butterflies, such as the small, powdery-blue spring azure, the beautiful purplish-black mourning cloak, the flashy white-and-orange Sara's orange tip, the cryptic brown-and-grey anglewings and the common tortoiseshell.

March is the month that birds begin to flood back into the Bella Coola Valley from southern British Columbia, Washington and Oregon. The northerly migrating birds that stay in the valley are known as summer residents. The red-breasted sapsucker, the flicker, the redwinged blackbird, the winter wren, the robin, the varied thrush and the song sparrow are among the first to arrive. They are joined by transient birds, known as visitors, that stop over on their northern migrations. It is as if a river of birds flows through the valley, washing the forest in melodic sound.

From the branches of a tall alder tree falls a bird song foreign to my ear. It's a pleasing medley of disjointed warbles and whistles. I look closely and see a grey-and-black, robin-sized bird, with a conspicuous long tail. The bird looks my way, to reveal a black mask and a stout, sharply hooked bill. A northern shrike—a bird headed for the far north, and a rare sighting in the Bella Coola Valley. The northern shrike is one of nature's more unusual experiments, for it is the only true predator that has evolved from songbirds to actively hunt small birds, mice and other mammals. A shrike will typically engage in a long chase before knocking a songbird to the ground, killing it with a peck to the skull. It will sometimes impale its victim on a thorn branch or even on a barbed-wire fence, before eating it, a practice that has earned it the nickname butcher bird. Above the tree line, in the distance, a chorus of loud, sonorous bugle notes signals the movement of a flock of large, white swans flying in V formation. Their flight is characterized by deep, ponderous wing beats, their necks fully extended. The trumpeter swan is the largest waterfowl in North America, reaching up to 2 metres and weighing over 9 kilograms.

The swans are on their way up valley to feed on grass and grass roots in a ranch field. Across from me a majestic, mature bald eagle lands heavily on the brittle branch of an old snag. The branch breaks and the eagle carries it off to add it to its massive, cup-shaped nest near the top of a large, old black cottonwood that looks down on the river.

On the coast, bald eagles prefer to build their nests in the broken tops of tall, large-diameter coniferous trees, particularly Sitka spruce and Douglas fir. Because of logging, those trees are vanishing, forcing nesting eagles to shift to black cottonwoods. In the last few years the cottonwoods up and down the Bella Coola Valley have come under attack as people chop them down for quick cash. Residents find it difficult to resist the urge to liquidate the huge, old cottonwoods on their property, which fetch $25 per cubic metre, and there are no regulations to prevent people from chopping them down. Nobody seems to be asking: When the big cottonwoods are gone, where will the bald eagles nest?

Often when you go fishing in the Bella Coola Valley the journey to the river turns out to be a lot longer than expected. But then the heavy splash of a fish or the steady rustling of the current reminds you of what you've come for. Downstream, where the Salloomt River flows into the Bella Coola, my attention is drawn to the water by a noisy flock of twenty common mergansers, excitedly quacking and thrashing about as they feed on salmon fry. Mergansers are specialists in catching fish. They snap up panic-stricken juvenile fry that are darting around in the shallows. In deeper water mergansers dive and use their wings and feet to chase down fish up to 25 centimetres long. They take bigger fish if they get the chance. A friend once found a dead merganser that had choked on a 45-centimetre trout; it had bitten off more than it could swallow. The bill of the merganser is long, narrow and lined with backward-pointing serrations, which help the bird grip slippery fish. When large numbers of fry are in the river, mergansers form lines that work together to drive juvenile fish to the shallows.

The merganser is not alone at the mouth of the Salloomt River. A great blue heron is wading through the shallows, slowly pondering its options—then striking with amazing speed. A belted kingfisher hovers over the smooth water, chatters in a harsh, staccato voice, and then plunges, shattering the surface.

A dipper searches among rocks for hiding fry. In the distance, a river otter gallops through a shallow pool, sending off a spray of water as it snaps up tiny salmon.

It's time to be fishing. As I look into the clear waters of Snootli Creek, chum fry seem everywhere. There are sparkling schools of fish moving downstream towards the Bella Coola River ahead of me. I can see fry along the edges of the creek, trapped in small puddles, and in some places there are even fry trapped under ice. The fry can't get free, but they are still alive— gill covers pulse and their bodies occasionally twitch. As the day warms and the stream levels rise, the trapped fish will make their way back into Snootli Creek. A few of the chum fry have their adipose fins clipped, marking them as coming from the Snootli Hatchery. Each year, some two million chum fry are released into Snootli Creek in March to join the larger schools of wild fish that are migrating to the sea.

Chum fry are the first smolts to migrate out of the Bella Coola River system. Typically, chum smolt migration peaks in the week of March 19 to 26. Then follows the emergence of the pink fry, the coho, the chinook, the cutthroat, the sockeye and the steelhead smolts. By mid-July all smolting fry have moved out of the system.

In the estuary the juvenile chum congregate in large schools and feed heavily on chironomids, amphipods and copepods. After a time they make their way down Burke Channel and eventually head out to the open Pacific. They will spend three or four years there before returning to the Bella Coola to spawn. Chum grow rapidly in the ocean, and when they return to the home of the big dog salmon, with hooked jaws and broad tails, they will average 4.5 kilograms and 76 centimetres long. Many will be much larger.

Despite all the activity at the mouth of Snootli Creek, there still is no sign of the Dolly Varden I've come looking for. I tie a small streamer, shaped and coloured like a chum fry, to the end of a short leader and cast diagonally, out across the mouth of Snootli into the Bella Coola River. The line starts to swing downstream, and almost instantly there is a swirl in the water. The line goes tight, and there is a fierce tug, a dogged pull that grows stronger as the rod bends and I try to pull the fish in. It dives and runs across towards the shore below me, using the force of the current to gain momentum. It jerks sharply—not fighting smoothly as a rainbow might. I bend the rod deeply and hold it there. The line thrums against the current, fixed to an unmoving fish that has gone to the bottom and may have braced itself against the rocks with flared pectoral fins. After a moment, I tilt the rod to one side. The change of angle forces the fish to move. It comes up in a rush, swirls near the surface, showing a broad silver flank, and dives again. This time it doesn't quite make it to its hiding place on the bottom. I can feel it twisting back and forth. After a few minutes it comes in. I know it's a Dolly Varden by the flash of colour from its spots. It seems to glare at me, its mouth clamped firmly around the fly. It's a nice fish of about 50 centimetres, maybe 1.5 kilograms. The fly comes out easily and the char turns back to the safety of the river with a thrash of its tail.

As I false-cast I wonder if the commotion has frightened whatever other Dolly Varden may be schooled there. There is no need to worry. The next cast is interrupted just as the second was. Working down through the pool I hook a fish, or feel a jarring strike, on almost every cast. The Dolly Varden are locked on to chum fry, and they instinctively slash at the fly every time it passes near them. Some days they are too busy with fry to take an artificial one, but the emergence is just beginning and their choice is limited. Today there are no really big fish, nothing over 1.1 kilograms, but later a spin fisher tells me of hitting some char over 2.2 kilograms farther downsteam. Maybe the big fish were running together—or maybe my light fly was drifting too high in the water column. The small fish make for a fine day nonetheless. And out of deference for the dead Dolly Varden I saw on the bank earlier, I release all I catch.

Late in the afternoon, as I turn to go, I see that the ice has melted just enough to release the imprisoned fry. I wonder if one of those ice salmon might take my fly in the years ahead, when I fish the returning run. In the home of the Big Dogs, you expect such miracles.

April

Moon for Making Eulachon Nets

The world smelled different today and on the hillsides the shadings had begun to change, with purples and greens seeping into the monochrome of winter. The sky was broken in half—a deep blue vastness lay directly over Bella Coola, so clear it seemed as if you were staring into the heart of space itself. To the east was a rich, textured blanket of white clouds. The weather front stood still, with hardly a movement of wind. But you could detect spring. Mixed with the smell of the sea was the scent of the earth thawing, the pungency of skunk cabbages and of eulachons rotting in pits across the river. Gently emerging and soon to overwhelm those earthy smells—the scent of the first blossoms on willow, saxifrage, salmonberry and wild currant.

As I breathe in the air of the valley I can't help but wonder what it all smells like to the bears that are stirring now in their mountain dens. With their powerful olfactory senses, surely it is the scent of the forest that makes them roll over and blink their eyes in the darkness of that first awakening.

Driving up the valley you can see emaciated deer feeding hungrily wherever succulent, new vegetation is showing. Most deer lose 30 per cent of their body weight over the winter months, and in April they browse with abandon, ignoring traffic on the nearby roads. The biting frost that has crusted the fields has suddenly gone, and in the muck last year's seeds are germinating, fungal mycelia are dividing, and plant rootlets are growing. Leaves of willows, black cottonwood, buckbrush, red-osier dogwood, salmonberry and wild currants are starting to show as a faint green halo on the branches. The foliage of the alder, birch, hazelnuts and sweet gale is not yet out, but swollen, protein-rich catkins give the outer branches of these plants a deep red glow. Locally this is known as "the purpling of the hills," for great swaths of the plants cover the lower slopes, giving the mountains a burgundy tinge.

Busy within the upper soil layer now are the worms, beetles and other insects that stirred with the thaw and have been pushed to the surface by the spring rains. It is not a coincidence that many of the first birds back to the valley—robins, juncos, song sparrows, red-winged blackbirds, winter wrens—are ground feeders that hop and flit across the forest floor, feeding on exposed seeds and turning the litter cover to find insects.

Along the river the ice has retreated, fully exposing the gravel bars. When April showers sweep up the valley you see the pale grey rocks turning dark as the downpour approaches. Then a cold rain is on you, rattling the willow branches.

On clear days the valley is stunningly beautiful, with the mountains glaring in a snow cover that reaches to just below the tree line. As the days lengthen and warm, the snow line retreats raggedly—and far below, the river slowly rises.

The Nuxalk call April Siqyulc, the Moon for Making Eula-chon Nets. For years I could not understand why they called it that, because by April the main eulachon run had ended. But Native names are almost always literal, and I knew that some-where in the past there must have been a reason for them to build nets so late in the spring. Then an elder solved the mystery. Long ago, near the beginning of his memory, there had been a second run of eulachon that arrived after the first run had passed. While the stink boxes were ripening, a new wave of fish came in. So the people made hand nets and refreshed their supply.

But those late-running eulachons have disappeared. Nobody knows why. And only the oldest can remember the runs of late April. They are still waiting for them to return.

For the moment the river is in perfect condition for fly-fishing—low and clear. By early April many of the Dolly Varden have dropped down the river with the descending schools of chum fry, but some remain and they are joined by remnant runs of spring steelhead. What draws me to the river now is a vora-cious, powerful and beautiful species of trout that seems to have been put on the planet for anglers. When sea-run cutthroat go on the feed they will take just about any kind of lure thrown at them. They are so aggressive at times that they ignore the fum-bling casts of even the most clumsy angler and rise to take flies that would have startled any other fish. Because the sea-run cutthroat is such an easily caught fish, its numbers have declined dramatically throughout the Pacific Northwest. In British Colum-bia stocks are so low that in most coastal areas it is illegal to kill any wild cutthroat. In the Bella Coola—perhaps once the great-est sea-run stream in the world—there are still many cutthroat, but not as many. On an April day it is possible to find runs where trout porpoise and roll all around the boat. But the old-timers say those pools are scattered now, where once the whole river boiled with sea-run trout, as they fed on emerging masses of pink salmon fry.

Of all the stocks in the Bella Coola system the one that continues to thrive is pink salmon, whose emergence in April so excites the cutthroat. In fact, pinks outnumber all other salmon and trout species combined by a ratio of 10 to 1. The target escapement of pinks into the Bella Coola system is 1 million fish, but the average annual return is well over 1.5 million—giving the river a surplus of 5 million over the past decade. There are many reasons pinks are so successful. They have a short life cycle—two years—so they mature sooner and spawn more often than other salmon. Pinks also spend very little time in fresh water, so they are not as vulnerable to habitat degradation. And because their flesh is not as prized as that of some of the other salmon, the economic incentive to slaughter them is not as strong.

Pink salmon are hugely important to the ecology of the valley. Each year spawning pinks will deposit an average of 800 million eggs into the gravels of the Bella Coola River. In an average year, 61 million fry will emerge. Consider for a moment the richness of what the pinks bring to the Bella Coola, to be consumed by everything from steelhead to salamanders: approximately 1.5 million kilograms of adult pink salmon flesh is left after the spawn; 117,000 kilograms of eggs are deposited, and 8000 kilograms of fry emerge to be greeted by the clattering call of gulls and the slashing attacks of trout and other predators.

The pinks provide a stunning enrichment of the valley, and in April, when they drift downstream in schools, the fry migration triggers one of the greatest trout fisheries on the river.

The Junction Pool, where the Atnarko and Talchako join to form the Bella Coola River, is a good place to go searching for

April cutthroat because of the pink fry that pour down into it from the Atnarko, but it is a place that resonates with danger. When I think of Junction Pool, I see the massive head of a grizzly bear and hear the pop its teeth make when its jaws swivel shut. Later in the month the air there will be rich with the scent of wildflowers, but for me it is also tinged with the musty, unsettling scent of bear.

On the way to Junction Pool the highway curves gently along a bend in the river known as Canoe Crossing. It is hard to pass without stopping to study the surface of this deep pool. And once you've done that it only seems to make sense to take out your fly rod and scramble down the steep bank to test the water. Just to see.

The route to the river crosses a small beaver dam built on a side stream. Above the wickerwork of willow branches, stones and mud, the creek has formed into a series of pools that provides ideal rearing habitat for trout and salmon. But the dam and a series of similar structures above it also make it difficult for the fish to move upstream or downstream. Each year more and more vegetation invades the margins of the sloughlike creek, and more beavers build dams, which effectively block any migration of the cutthroat.

By cutting down the conifers and allowing alder and other deciduous trees to flourish in the valley bottom, humans have provided beavers with a seemingly endless source of food. The killing of large carnivores (wolves and cougars) that prey on beaver has also benefited beavers over the years. Not surprisingly, the local beaver population has exploded, as it has in many valleys on the coast, leading to complaints about plugged culverts and flooded farmlands. It is a reminder of how humans have an unintended but profound impact on nature.

Below the beaver dam at Canoe Crossing the creek melds with the bigger water of the river, creating a seam in the current that cutthroat like to hold in. They are here waiting for spring rains to raise the water level so that they can pass into the side streams to spawn. Many have been holding in the pool for months.

Like most anadromous fish, maturing sea-run cutthroat do not have to feed while in fresh water and, despite their easy reputation, can prove difficult to catch. But they seem helplessly addicted to pink fry and will feed heavily once the emergence begins.

Unfortunately for the species, the largest cutthroat are the most vulnerable. When bait is drifted through a pool, the first cutthroat to bite are often those with the highest social rank— the most aggressive, the largest and genetically "the most fit" individuals. Smaller members of the school will subsequently move into the vacated lies after the dominant fish are killed, and they will be the ones that ultimately secure the best spawning gravels. By killing the largest cutthroat, then, anglers inadvertently select for smaller, less aggressive fish.

When the water from melting snowpacks floods the creek later in spring, the mature cutthroat move out of Canoe Crossing to pass over the beaver dams. There and in other tributaries along the main stem, the females will spawn several times each, laying about a thousand eggs. Spawning takes place during the day and night, and the fish are typically out of the system in two or three days.

In the Bella Coola, cutthroat spawn between March and June, with most activity occurring in May. Although adult sea-run cutthroat have been taken as far up the system as the Atnarko River at Stillwater Lake, some 100 kilometres from the ocean, most are found in the lower Bella Coola Valley.

After spawning, the spent sea-run cutthroat seek quiet waters in the river, where they begin feeding again on aquatic insects, sculpins, fry and juvenile salmon or trout. If they are lucky, they will live to spawn again. Unlike salmon, which all die after spawning, up to 40 per cent of sea-run cutthroat survive spawning.

Sea-runs, so called because they make annual sojourns to the ocean, feed heavily in salt water on euphausiids, gammarid amphipods, isopods, three-spined sticklebacks, Pacific sand lance, shrimp, sculpins, anchovies and herring. Some winter in salt water; some stray into neighbouring streams. The majority of mature sea-runs return to the Bella Coola River by August or September, holding over to spawn. At times the fish become restless and make migrations up and down the river.

Sea-run cutthroat are easy to catch when they first return to the river because they retain the aggressive feeding patterns set at sea. But—like salmon and steelhead—they generally stop feeding soon after entering fresh water. In spring, sea-run cutthroat revert to their aggressive feeding ways, in which they will take almost anything—particularly anything that looks like a small fish. In March and April, almost all trout caught contain large quantities of pink or chum fry. It is not unusual to clean a cutthroat and find sixty fry in its stomach.

The pool at Canoe Crossing has long been popular with Bella Coola anglers. Over the years far too many trout have been killed there and at the other places where the fish are known to hold. Until recently, however, few of those who fished in the valley ever thought there would be a shortage of cutthroat.

The late Miguel Moreno, a pastor who loved horses and trout fishing, once recounted a typical trip to the pool, in 1982, when a friend discovered where the sea-run cutthroat were wintering:

"He called me and we went together; by then he had been going every day and already had his freezer packed with cutthroats. The limit then was eight fish a day. We parked on the highway and he showed me from on top of the bank something that almost choked me; down below in the water ... more than eighty huge cutthroats were moving slowly around the big boulders just beside the bank. They would probably average two and a half pounds. My friend fished with worms and a little bobber, and I used a little #10 Colorado spinner, silver, and we both got our limit in no time, even releasing those who were less than eighteen inches. The fish were all silver and good fighters.

"Since then and after several floods, the river and the bank have changed considerably, and although still you can find some cutthroats in the run of the main river, in front of the bend of the highway, the fishing today has nothing to do with what I enjoyed then. What I really regret is that I was not yet converted to fly-fishing; it could have been some experience to fly-fish this hole then."

Schools of eighty trout aren't seen in the Canoe Crossing pool now. But it is still a wonderful place to fish. On a bright April morning using a sink tip line and 3-foot leader, I tie on a fry imitation known as a Rolled Muddler to search the water. The Canoe Crossing pool is deep and the fish typically lie near the rocky bottom. The sink tip helps take the fly down. After stringing up the rod, I scan the river and just upstream, in an eddy created where the faster water begins to slow, I see the familiar surface swirl of a cutthroat slashing at fry. Sometimes it looks like the trout are feeding on the surface, but they are surging after fish in the top several centimetres of water. Typically, cutthroat will charge through a pod of drifting fry and then turn back for the injured fish. A single fly, fished dead drift or retrieved with an occasional twitch so that it seems hurt, will almost always be attacked.

I wade knee deep to cast the fly across and slightly upstream. For a few minutes I just work the line out, leading it back and forth with the rod, enjoying the sensation of it flying over the river. Then I drive the rod forward, release the line and feel it shoot out through the guides. The fly settles far out on a bright piece of water, then sinks and starts to swim. As the line swings across below me, the current lifts the fly towards the surface. The rising motion is irresistible to trout. One strikes suddenly, boiling just beneath the surface. I lift the rod and feel the solidness of it. When it comes in, I see it's a lovely female fish of just over a kilogram. This time of year maturing cutthroat are beautifully spotted above and below the lateral line, with black splashes of pigment scattered over olive-green backs that blend with the green algae on the river stones. The fish has a soft pink blush on its cheeks, a characteristic that often makes novice anglers think they've caught a rainbow. Unlike the pink of a rainbow, however, a cutthroat's pink colour doesn't extend along the sides in bands. Under the jaw is a sure sign that the fish is a cutthroat: two blood-red slashes, which give the fish its name.

The red streaks are thought to play a role in determining social rank. When cutthroat of roughly equal size meet, they may face one another, arch their backs, lower their dorsal fins, open their gills wide and then flare the throat to show the red streaks. If that doesn't settle things, they may fight to determine which is superior.

I quickly release the fish and lay out another cast to the same spot, knowing that cutthroat often run in schools. After the line straightens, I begin to strip the line in slowly but with an occasional erratic twitch—an attempt to imitate the movements of a wounded fry. Suddenly there's a slashing take. The line is drawn tight through the current. In the depths the trout's silvery-white sides glint as it darts for cover. There is a jump or two, high up, with the fish crashing back on its tail, and then the trout tires. It is a twin of the first fish, just a couple of centimetres longer. Often you will catch fish after fish like this, all seemingly made from the same mold.

There are no further strikes until I work my way downstream about 15 metres and hit the main pack of fish. Four casts, four fish. All about a kilogram. Then the action dies.

As I ponder a change of flies, a song sparrow, a small chocolate-brown bird with a grey stripe above its eyes, emerges from the willow thickets nearby, alights on a stick, throws back its head and begins to sing. From the old-growth Douglas fir forest behind me, I can hear the nasal *yack-yack-yack* of a red-breasted nuthatch—sounding much like a child's small tin horn. Life is surging through the valley now, as it is all along the Pacific coast, as successive waves of birds return. From deep within the knotted branches of a large spruce tree I hear for the first time this year the *tee-tee-tee* of the ruby-crowned kinglet. And from high in one of the old cottonwood trees a flicker calls and starts to hammer on a dead, hollow, resonating limb. Males drum to claim territory in the spring and to summon mates.

Across the river a flock of male red-winged blackbirds falls down in a shower of glistening black feathers. When the bachelor flocks first arrive in early April, most of the inland marshes are still frozen. For the next few weeks they will be companions along the river, but as soon as it warms enough to open the marshes, they will move on.

With the rod cradled in the crook of my elbow and the

leader lying across the palm of my hand, I ponder the Rolled Muddler. The brown, deer-hair body has been torn apart by the sharp teeth of the trout, and a strand of golden tinsel that covered the shank of the hook has begun to unravel. As I search in my fly box for a replacement, a large bumblebee blunders past, hovering for a moment over my bright red coat. It is the first I have seen this year—and it drones through air currents increasingly rich with scent. By the middle of month the valley will be filled with the sweet smell of cottonwood buds and mountain ash flowers. And by month's end a profusion of wild orchids and coastal lilies will have added their fragrance. Much of the olfactory signals or "news" broadcast by the flowering plants is designed to attract pollinators such as the bumblebee. In April, bees, syrphid flies, butterflies, moths and beetles come out of their winter hiding places and begin pollinating early-season flowers.

The lone bumblebee is undoubtedly a queen, fresh from her hibernation burrow. She's in search of food or a place to establish a new colony. Unlike honeybees, in which the entire colony of queen, workers and drones overwinter, bumblebee colonies die out each fall, and it is up to a lone, surviving queen to establish a new colony. At night she will roost under moss and other vegetation; by day she will eat all the pollen and nectar she can find. Once she has built her energy reserves, she'll look for a place to lay her eggs. Bumblebees often move into the old nests of small mammals or birds.

The bee drones off into a stream bank willow thicket, not pointlessly wandering, but drawn by the fragrant pussy willows —one of the first flowers of the year. The wind stirs. If you could capture the air today and look at it under a microscope you'd find the sky full of countless pollen particles released by conifer trees, alders, trembling aspens, black cottonwoods, paper birch and the various willows. Later in the season pollen from grasses, sedges and stinging nettle fills the air.

I knot on a new fly, but before I can get another chance at the pool, I'm joined by the first of an apparently endless stream of local catch-and-kill anglers. Word is out that the cutthroat are feeding. Among anglers there seems to be a process that works something like wind pollination—in which news of good fishing spreads through the community as if on magic air currents.

Most of the river is deserted today, but the known holding pools will all be visited by anglers. An elderly man and his young grandson rattle down the roadside bank to join me on the gravel bar.

"Would you mind if we fished for a while?" asks the old man, who's dressed in a rough wool sweater, blue jeans and work boots. The boy looks on eagerly, his eyes as dark and shining as the river.

"Of course not. I've had my turn; you go ahead," I say. Over the next half-hour while I watch from my drift-log seat, the fly rod resting across my knees, he kills twelve cutthroat, some 50 centimetres long, using a small ball of roe wrapped around a weighted hook. Free-drifted with the current, the bait cannot pass through the pool without a strike. His grandson, who is about seven years old, soon catches on and hooks and kills two cutthroat of his own. Their expressions are memorable; they both are enjoying this fishing experience immensely. I know both will cherish the memories of the morning together for many years ahead. The last fish the old man catches is a beautiful doe steelhead, the first I have seen in over a year. It is killed as well, clubbed over the head with a stone. There is nothing illegal about what they have done. Although steelhead are protected on the Bella Coola and there is a two-trout-a-day limit for cutthroat, they are both Natives and as such are exempt from fishing regulations. They can kill what they want, when they want, how they want.

The argument made to justify this is simple: the Native people have a historical right to the fish, and if their harvest raises environmental concerns, it is only because the much larger non-Native population has overfished and caused habitat damage. Whatever weight that argument has, however, it fails to address the fundamental concern—which is that cutthroat and steelhead populations are in decline. A dead fish does not care if it is killed by a white or a Native hand—and has no better chance of spawning. Blame is not the issue—survival is.

As the elderly man and his grandson leave with their dead fish strung on willow branches, two long-time valley residents arrive and begin fishing on the south side of the river, which they've reached by following a logging road. Both are descendants of original European settlers. They too have a good day, casting gobs of roe out into the river. Within twenty minutes, they catch and kill their limit of cutthroat and one lands a steelhead. The big silvery fish is dragged onto the shore, its body thumping powerfully against the stones. One of them steps on the fish to stop it from thrashing about. For several minutes the two admire the steelhead and debate what they should do. Should they kill it, which would make them poachers, or should they release it, which to them seems wasteful? In the end, one of the anglers pulls out a camera and photographs his partner holding a suffocating steelhead by its tail. A glop of slime and water drips from its nose. The fish is thrown back. As it floats downstream, struggling weakly to right itself, a bald eagle, attracted by a white flash of belly, swoops from a high cottonwood and, with a thrashing of wings, lifts the steelhead from the surface. I hear the anglers swearing bitterly. I know they will never release another steelhead, having now confirmed their suspicions that catch-and-release simply does not work.

Just as they leave a drift boat comes into sight and quickly moves to the head of the pool. There are two clients in the boat with a professional guide, drawn by the scent of fish. As I make my way back up to the road I hear the call: "Fish on!" Casting roe, they will catch and release a dozen cutthroat before moving on to the next pool. Almost half their catch will die because they will be hooked deeply in the throat. Numerous studies involving thousands of fish have shown that 30 to 40 per cent of trout caught with bait die after release. In contrast, only 4 per cent of trout caught on flies are mortally wounded. But the government shies away from bait bans, saying it does not want to pander to elitist fly-fishing anglers.

Although there are runs in the river that few people know about and that still roll heavy with fish, the future of the Bella Coola sea-run cutthroat does not look good. As recently as twenty years ago, one could catch-and-release eighty trout in one day. Now that would make a good year. There may have been as many as ten thousand sea-run cutthroat in the system when Europeans first settled in the valley. Every creek had a resident population of spawning cutthroat, but now few have enough to support a fishery. In early spring sea-runs were found everywhere in a main river—under the cutbanks, in the bright riffles and beneath the logjams. Now the schools are mainly found in a dozen or so pools throughout the river—pools that are well known to anglers.

In the spring of 1993, two researchers spent April and May

looking for spawning cutthroat in the Bella Coola system. Streams were walked and weirs were placed across some streams to capture spawning adults. The project cost the government over $20,000—but only about fifty spawning pairs were found, suggesting there were far fewer cutthroat than anyone had ever guessed.

The number of big fish has dropped dramatically too. Two decades ago it was common to encounter cutthroat over 2 kilograms. Now such large fish are rare. Graham Hall, one of the first fly-fishers to settle in the valley, doesn't get out on the water anymore because of his age. But he recalls the way it used to be. He turns off his big television set to talk.

His story winds its way through the history of the valley, the hanging bridge that got washed out, the cougar hunter who became a game warden, and then, finally, he gets to talking about fishing in paradise:

"It was 1965 or 1966, at the mouth of Thorsen Creek, and I was looking for coho. Thorsen Creek and Skimlik Creek consisted of seven or eight little streams in those days. A beautiful area of big firs, cedars, hemlocks growing all through there. I don't know how forestry allowed logging to take place in the area, but they did. The logging destroyed the whole area. Nowadays Thorsen Creek is all shallow, washed out.

"Anyway, I had made up some flies that were similar to a General Money fly, but instead of the orange wings it had yellow wings. I hooked up my fly rod and started casting out into the water. Just letting the fly drift down in the creek. First cast, wham! and I thought, 'Oh, God!' I gotta coho right away. The fish fought like a steelhead. I pulled the fish in. A real beautiful silver bright fish. It turned out to be a big sea-run cutthroat fresh from the sea. But I had never seen such a big cutthroat, so I wasn't sure what it was when I first saw it. I continued to fish, and every cast I made I hooked one of these big fish. Altogether I must have landed five or six of them in there. I figured I would take two of these home so I would have some for supper. In those days, I did have a bit of a family to feed. When I brought these fish home, Skate Haynes, the game warden, was there, and so I asked him, 'What the heck are these fish? They are not rainbow trout. They are not steelhead. And they are not salmon.' Because they just came out of the salt water, they still had sea lice on them; they were chrome-silver and you could not see the orange slash under the throat yet. So Skate checked them out. Weighed them. Took some of the scales, Counted the fin rays. They were cutthroat. Skate could not believe it either; he said 'Gosh, it is the biggest cutthroat I have ever seen.' One weighed in at seven pounds, the other just over six pounds. All the other ones I caught would have come in well over five pounds.

"In those days, I never saw anyone else fishing that stretch of the river. The fishing was so fabulous. A fly-fisherman's dream. And it's gone, it's all shot now. The odd trout goes in there now, but nothing like the old days."

Hall was a bit of an oddity on the river in those days because he fished with a fly rod—not just for trout but for steelhead and salmon too. And he was unusual in that he practised catch-and-release long before it came into vogue. Big trout were common, he said. You could expect a 2-kilogram trout anytime. His biggest was 4.5 kilograms, taken on a Sofa Pillow dry fly. But as the years passed there were fewer and fewer big fish.

"We lost those big ones," he says sadly. He thinks they were fished out by Native nets, strung at the mouth of the river. But certainly many were killed by sports anglers too. Trophy fish—genetic treasures—eradicated by those who valued them most.

"Beautiful. Just like paradise. The sort of thing you dream of," Hall says wistfully of those early fly-fishing days. Before turning the baseball game back on, he thanks his visitors for coming to talk about fish. For reminding him how it once was.

Earlier I had floated a long reach of the Bella Coola, getting out to cast in runs where few people fish. There were riffles stacked with cutthroat, where twenty trout could be seen slashing at fry. But the biggest fish were just over a kilogram and most were close to a kilogram, about 45 centimetres long.

There are many reasons for the decline of the Bella Coola sea-run cutthroat. Their biology puts them at risk. There is limited spawning habitat, and much has been destroyed by agricultural, residential and logging development. Damage to small streams is widespread and shocking in its extent for such a remote valley. And commercial salmon fishers have accidentally killed cutthroat in Burke Channel and Fitz Hugh Sound. But there can be no doubt that sports anglers have done considerable harm too. Numerous studies have shown that stream-dwelling cutthroat are highly vulnerable. In one small Idaho stream 50 per cent of all catchable-sized cutthroat trout were harvested in only thirty-two hours of angling effort. It is not surprising that sea-run cutthroat populations have undergone major declines in the past fifteen to twenty years throughout most of the Pacific Northwest. It is an old story that has been played out all along the coast—and that has now come to threaten the sea-runs at the heart of their stronghold—in the Bella Coola.

It's late in the month now and driving up to Junction Pool I go looking for a last April cutthroat. Soon the pink outmigration will be over and the river will start to rise. Passing Canoe Crossing, I see that the pool is deserted. Word is out that the fishing has not been good there the past few days. Perhaps the fish have moved on. Perhaps they have all been killed. But they will be holding at the Junction Pool. I know that. I can smell that they are there.

The valley is filled with the sweet scent of cottonwood buds and touched by the fragrance of wild yellow violets and coastal orchids. The trail to Junction Pool is a pretty walk but one that always spooks me. At the head of the trail are large signs left over from last summer warning of roving grizzly bears. The bears come here to fish for big chinooks in August—and so do anglers from all over North America. Often the anglers leave blood and guts along the riverbank when they clean their catch. The bears smell it. Last year a young male grizzly charged a group of anglers here. They ran, leaving a pile of freshly caught salmon behind. Something clicked inside the bear's head, and throughout the summer, whenever it saw anglers, it made bluff charges to get more fish.

Walking the trail, I see no sign of bear. No evidence of overturned rocks, rotten trees torn apart, no clawed or rubbed bark, fresh diggings or trampled vegetation, dead animals or dead fish. But somehow the air seems charged; it's as if the forest is hiding something.

Far above me, from the bluffs across the river, I can hear the hooting call of a male blue grouse. The alder thickets also echo with the drumming of a cock ruffed grouse—sounding like a distant, muffled engine that stutters to a start and then accelerates before coming to an abrupt stop.

Bup ... bup ... bup ... bup ... bup-bup-bup-up—r-rr, it goes, making the woods vibrate and underscoring the sexual urgency of spring.

The surface of Junction Pool is slick and shows no sign of trout when I arrive. But I know they have to be there. The Atnarko pumps out more pinks than any other tributary and fry were still drifting down. Wading out, using a dry line to sweep a minnow imitation across the shallow tail of the pool, I soon have a strong strike. After a brief fight a solid cutthroat of about 45 centimetres comes to hand. It may have been a resident cutthroat, that is, a trout that had spent its entire year in the river. Fishery biologists believe that resident cutthroat are more likely to be found in the Atnarko River and are more likely to spawn in tributaries farther upstream than sea-run cutthroat. The fish was fat and looked to be full of fry. I had caught and killed a similar one here two years ago, and when I cleaned it I counted seventy-six pink and two chum fry. With a quick twist of the hook, I set the trout free.

As I kneel in the shallows, the river lapping gently around me, I hear a branch snap and the sound, although it is faint, cuts through everything. It separates itself from the gentle cottonwood brushing of branch against branch, from the soft rustling of grasses in the wind and from the murmur of water. It brings my head up. There, directly across the river, planted solidly on the water's edge, is a subadult grizzly. I reel in.

The ratchet of the reel or the movement of the rod makes him look directly at me—and then rise on his hind legs. His forepaws hang down as if weighted on the tips. Bears stand up to get a better view, not to attack—but it is an action that sends a jolt through your nervous system. The bear had looked big, but now it appears huge and the shallows across the tail of the pool seem diminished.

I move to a half-crouch, preparing to back out of the water. The fly has been reeled in until it snagged in the top eye of the rod. I look back over one shoulder, calculating. Ten yards to shore. A hard scramble up the cutbank in chest waders. Then the trail through the woods. The truck seems a long, long way off. I look for a tree to climb.

The bear makes a woofing sound, rough and doglike but not like anything I've ever heard before. After a moment it drops to all fours, lowers its dish-shaped head, flattens its ears and stares at me. What do I look like in those weak brown eyes? The wind plays on its fur. Suddenly it pops its jaws and growls from somewhere deep in its throat. The growl of a bear runs up your spine and comes to rest at the base of your skull, where a door opens into a dark, instinctive place that is as old as the Bella Coola River itself. I can taste the charge coming.

Usually Bella Coola grizzly bears run off once they see people. But this was probably the same young bear that had chased anglers here last summer. He was fresh from his den, remembering. A bear like this is said to be habituated to humans and is not far removed from being a killer.

I am frozen, not wanting this to happen. If I run, he will chase. I could drop my pack, my rod, shake off my jacket. The cottonwoods would be hard to climb, but if he stopped to paw through my gear, I would have a chance.

It is amazing how fast a bear can move. Once on the Copper River, in the Queen Charlotte Islands, I was charged by a black bear. It ambled down the beach across from me, leisurely swam the river, then put down its head and came with great, bounding, toe-to-heel strides that brought it on like a speeding car. Luckily a boat was only a few steps away.

Before the grizzly decides what to do, two anglers come into sight on the riverbank above me. They are talking noisily as they come, their voices sounding alien over the language of the river. The bear wheels instantly and crashes off into the bushes, which is the way most bears react, most of the time. The anglers watch the bear run, then start to fish, throwing spinners out into the pool.

Going back up the trail I notice the first bright orchids unfolding. I don't have to bend low to smell them. The scent seems to go right into my lungs, into my blood.

May

~

Moon for
Making Salmon Weirs

Harvey and I have lost the creek that was guiding us through the forest. It is somewhere west, screened by the old-growth fir trees that can be found in the tag end of Tweedsmuir Park, near Burnt Bridge. It's here that Mackenzie came down out of the Rainbow Mountains with a small group of hardened men, two hundred years ago, following the Grease Trail, on his epic journey to the Pacific. He trod this path, like us, following the gradual slope of the land towards the Bella Coola River. He came seeking a trade route; we are searching for something just as elusive and perhaps just as imaginary: a fish with a pale, silt-green back as slick as silk that is part salmon, part myth.

Until recently, March and April were among the best times to fish for steelhead in the Bella Coola River. But the run that sustained a once great sports fishery has virtually been eradicated. Now the best chance for a spring fish is in May, when the late-arriving remnants of the run slip in under the cover of coloured water.

We come to the river suddenly. It has not announced itself beforehand with the clashing sound of rapids. But there it is ahead through the forest, glinting gently in the early-afternoon sun. We follow along the bank for a while, staying in the trees, where the walking is easy on deep moss, passing a long, slow series of slick pools. Some tree trunks along the river have been shredded by bears, which have torn off bark to feed on the delicious sapwood that concentrates nutrients. The Nuxalk used to eat the inside of the bark of hemlock and cottonwood too. They would peel back the thick skin, scrape the sap with a knife and eat it, sweet and sticky, right off the blade.

It is warm and the river is rising, slowly staining with siltation. In a few weeks it will not be recognizable as the same river, becoming cloudy and secretive. For the moment it is still relatively clear, although the boulders in midstream are already fading to white.

Along the shore we see delicate little yellow stoneflies hatching and watch for the sign of rising fish. An occasional mayfly drifts past on the breeze, and upstream a dozen swallows are actively feeding, dipping and soaring above the river where a swarm of black flies is dancing. Mosquitoes attack us in the shade. In the woods we hear golden and white-crowned sparrows singing, part of an invasion of fly-catching birds migrating through the valley to nesting grounds in the subalpine. A large insect flutters clumsily over the water, drops to the surface, struggles in a tantalizing way, then makes a short flight before dropping again. It is a giant stonefly, nearly 5 centimetres long, which is the largest of its kind in North America. It has a dark brown back and a char red underbelly. Heavily veined, dark grey wings lie flat over its body. Stoneflies trigger violent underwater strikes and surface rises. When a hatch is on even the biggest, most wary fish come into play.

The nymphs can be fished upstream, in a dead drift, to imitate insects that have lost their footing and are drifting helplessly with the current. Or they can be worked downstream and across to the shoreline—to imitate migrating nymphs. Dry-fly imitations can be fished drag free, or with short skittering movements across the surface. Stoneflies are so clumsy in flight that a sloppy cast that splashes down hard will often provoke a strike, rather than spooking the fish.

There are no fish stirring, indicating the stonefly hatch is just beginning, but we know this is one of the few places, in all of this magnificent river, where steelhead are holding. And if anything will trigger an instinctive feeding reflex in a steelhead, it is the sight of an egg-laying giant stonefly fluttering on the water.

There once was a time when you could fish anywhere in the Bella Coola system in the spring and expect to encounter steelhead. The old-timers say, oh, you could just go out there and see them lying like stacked wood. You could catch as many as you wanted. Nothing to it. But for a week we have been drifting and wading the river, casting to empty runs and gliding over deserted pools.

A fisheries survey crew, swimming the river in wet suits, has found a few pockets of steelhead, confirming what we suspected, that they are spread thin. Here, in the upper Bella Coola, we know we will find whatever is left of what once was.

Steelhead are drawn to this section of the river by the easy current and the big boulders that litter the bottom, providing resting places until spawning time. Sometimes one of the big fish will detach itself from its hold, tilt up and take a stonefly. Sometimes they will just roll languidly, as if tasting the surface layer, exposing broad, silver flanks that exude a sense of immense power.

Over the years many large steelhead have been caught in the Bella Coola, including a legendary fish that came to a fly after a snowfall on March 29, 1976. That steelhead—41.75 inches (106 centimetres) long and 25 pounds, 2 ounces (about 11.5 kilograms), in weight—was taken by Gary Miltenberger on a Morning Magic, a silver-bodied streamer with wings of red and yellow.

Miltenberger had been set to fly out to a logging camp that morning, but a blizzard grounded the floatplane. So he went fishing, starting at a place called Otter Run, but then moving down because of other anglers, to fish a pool called Stump Hole.

"It was about 2:30 P.M.," he recalls. "About a third of the way down the Stump Hole I had a solid take. But the fish didn't jump like a lot of steelhead do, not even a roll or thrash on the surface. I felt several awesome surges that I've since learned are that of a big fish shaking its head, then several long, powerful runs upstream in swift, strong current. I'd never seen that before either; all the other ones had gone downstream. After about fifteen minutes of back-and-forth tug-o'-war I saw a broad tail at the surface, at least a foot across, and I knew I was into a very large fish. The memory of the battle is as vivid today, all these years later. He then decided he'd had enough time toying with me and headed down the run. I put on the pressure as hard as I could, and over the course of the next twenty minutes he took another good dozen strong, steady runs before he began to tire.

"I figure the battle lasted forty minutes start to finish. I never knew for certain whether I was going to beat him or not until he was finally laying on his side at the very end of the pool just prior to the rapids which runs into the long run behind the Hagensborg Store. My hands and legs were literally shaking at the end of the battle, as much from the tension of the battle as from tiring myself while tiring the fish. He was silver-bright, with some of the scales scraped from one side by a seal or sea lion."

The steelhead won the annual *Field and Stream* first-place fly-fishing award for 1976 in the rainbow trout category and helped cement the Bella Coola's reputation as a great fishing river. Many fly-fishers have made odysseys to the Bella Coola Valley after seeing a picture in a magazine of Miltenberger holding that enormous fish on the riverbank.

The largest steelhead ever taken from the Bella Coola may be the one caught by Andy Schooner in 1965. It was 28½ pounds (about 13 kilograms). Wilf Christensen was erroneously given credit for catching the fish on spinning gear, but in fact it was taken in Schooner's gill net.

Because of its reputation for big fish and lots of them, a tremendous sports fishery flourished on the Bella Coola, starting in the mid-1950s and lasting for nearly thirty years. For a time it may have been the best steelhead stream anywhere, even better than the world-famous Dean River, which lies in the next major drainage north and which has long been recognized as the world's finest steelhead river.

From 1986 to 1989 Bella Coola anglers enjoyed some of the greatest steelhead fishing imaginable. Everybody was out catching and killing steelhead in those days. The local sports fishers, the Nuxalk and the guides with their paying clients.

During the peak season—March and April—a steady procession of drift boats passed through the major steelhead pools, most dragging bags of salmon roe in which barbed hooks were buried. A gob of roe lets off a soft cloud of oil when you drop it in the water. It must smell of sex and fertility to the steelhead, which are waiting to spawn, and they will take it in their mouths willingly, even though they are not feeding.

During those days of heavy fishing no wintering fish was safe.

The Nuxalk used both net and rod-and-reel to kill their steelhead. Up until the late 1980s you could wander along the lower 6 kilometres of the Bella Coola and find as many as forty nets strung across the river. Some were set a hundred metres or so apart. Each net was strung almost halfway across the river, and they were strategically arranged, first from one bank, then the other, so that they overlapped, effectively blocking the entire river. Four days a week, Sunday through Thursday, the gaping, patient nets waited for the steelhead. A good netter would take 6 to 12 fish a day. It was common for a net owner to take 100 steelhead a season. Using roe and spinning rods, Native anglers reported killing up to 120 steelhead each. Some did both, "sports" fishing while their nets hung in the current.

Some Nuxalk used boats and drift nets, searching for fish that had slipped past the set nets and the fleet of sports anglers. In one infamous drift three men killed one hundred steelhead in a day, filling their small boat with dead fish. One hundred dead steelhead, all in a pile.

In an average season the Nuxalk reported killing 800 steelhead, though it is likely they took more; sports anglers caught 2500 and killed 650, releasing the rest. Several hundred of the bait-hooked steelhead would undoubtedly have died later. Locals did not always bother to record their catches. Some years, between them, the Native and sports anglers killed close to 3000 steelhead.

As soon as the high water came up, most the fishing ended. Driftwood, lifted from the gravel bars, tore out the nets and the water became far more difficult to fish for spin casters. It was here, at the tail end of the run, that a small segment of fish arrived and were able to slip through. Those fish today are the remnants, literally the tail end, of what once was a great run of steelhead.

Long before the intense fisheries of the 1980s took their toll, early settlers had done untold damage to steelhead stocks. In the 1920s and 1930s locals used to take a horse and buggy up to Burnt Bridge Creek to fish for small "brook" trout, which in fact were juvenile steelhead. The number of steelhead that spawned then must have been phenomenal, judging by early newspaper reports.

From the *Bella Coola Courier*, September 19, 1914:

> One day last week A. E. Hall, J. Hoage and Harry Burt of the Crossing took each his rod and line and made for the Kahylst River [Burnt Bridge] which is famous for its brook trout. The party returned to the Crossing the next day with no less than seven hundred and thirty-two fish. For several days the main diet of the people of the Crossing and Firvale was brook trout.

At its peak the Bella Coola had a population of 5000 to 10,000 steelhead. Even as late as 1988, about 3000 fish were returning. By 1990 the Bella Coola's steelhead fishery had begun to collapse. That year only 1200 fish survived to spawn. Some local anglers had warned a crash was coming, as had some of those visiting from the United States, who had seen such systematic abuse elsewhere and who felt the pressure on the fishery was unsustainable.

When the collapse did come many responded with denial. Some said one bad year didn't prove anything. Others loudly affirmed that the fish would be back. Even some fisheries biologists tried to dismiss the collapse as an aberration. They all had faith in the Bella Coola's greatness. But more bad news followed. And soon it became apparent that one of the world's greatest steelhead runs had been virtually wiped out.

In 1991 a survey crew for the British Columbia fish and wildlife section flew the Bella Coola during the early spring, when the water was low and clear. Hovering above the river they could see the fish easily—dark forms against the grey and green stones on the bottom. They counted 93 steelhead in a well-known holding area that usually contained 1000 or more fish. The total spawning escapement for the system that year was estimated at only 800 fish.

The government responded to the survey by implementing, for the first time, a steelhead catch-and-release regulation for the entire Bella Coola system. Such restrictions had long been in place on many rivers in British Columbia. But the Bella Coola had been exempt.

For the next few years the catch-and-release regulations remained in effect, but there were no signs of recovery. Steelhead stocks soon fell to fewer than 500 spawners. The Nuxalk, citing historical rights, continued to use nets and bait to fish for steelhead. But their catch rate reflected the state of the run—a good net operator took only 10 fish in an entire season, not 100 or more.

In February 1995 some concerned local anglers put on dry suits, slipped into the ice-cold waters and drifted down the Atnarko and into the Bella Coola River, just to see for themselves. In the stretch where 93 steelhead had been seen a few years earlier, they counted only 15 steelhead.

In February 1997 biologists found 51 steelhead. They swam the entire river, drifting through one jade-green pool after another, listening to the muffled undersound of the river, feeling the coldness of the water pressing in on their faces. Great tracts of the river lay empty. The few steelhead they did find were clustered together in two or three pools like refugees. It was no longer a question of a bad run or two—the Bella Coola steelhead were facing extinction.

Many people have been bewildered by the sudden and traumatic decline of the Bella Coola's steelhead. It has happened elsewhere, of course, but to happen in a remote, rich river like this seems incredible. Some biologists speculate that ocean conditions are to blame. The argument is impossible to refute, because nobody knows for sure and coastwide there has been a significant drop in the ocean survival rate of several salmon species. But if the ocean had suddenly become less productive, how could one explain the strong runs that some rivers continued to have? Were the Bella Coola steelhead and those from the nearby Dean River, which continued to flourish, not sharing the same ocean?

There is no question that many Bella Coola steelhead have been killed at sea, in commercial nets. As recently as the early 1960s, summer gill-netters were catching four or five steelhead kelts a day each—which would total about three thousand fish throughout the fleet. The kelts, mending from their exhaustive spawning odysseys, were thin and the flesh was always poor. Many were simply dumped overboard, dead. Early studies found up to 19 per cent of Bella Coola steelhead were repeat spawners, mostly females. The kelts are the toughest of all the fish—the survivors whose genetic material is so vital to the stock. The fleet almost eradicated them.

Not only were Bella Coola kelts caught in commercial nets, but later in the summer bright silver fish were intercepted in the coastal inlets. Many of those fish, it is now known, were headed for the Bella Coola.

Steelhead, which range far north and west in the Pacific, were also caught in Asian drift nets, which are ostensibly set for squid but which in reality catch anything that swims. One study has estimated that open-ocean drift nets incidentally kill 41 million marine animals every year, including salmon, seals, whales, sharks, marlin, dolphins, seabirds and turtles.

Ocean fisheries have had a devastating effect over a very long period. Habitat destruction is another factor that has worn away at the stocks for decades. But to explain the Bella Coola's recent collapse, we must come back to the river and the staggering collective impact of sports and Native fishers. By rod and by net, we simply have killed far too many steelhead in the river.

Throughout the '60s and '70s, access to the river and fishing technology increased dramatically. Native in-river nets—once made of stinging nettle fibre but now made of lighter, stronger nylon mesh—became more efficient, and drift boats made them easier to set and retrieve. Spinning gear and drift boats (which studies show increase an angler's catch threefold on the Bella Coola) became immensely popular. Even fly-fishing technology improved, so anglers could cast farther and fish deeper.

The sports catch limits on the Bella Coola were ridiculously high for decades. Some old-timers tell of legally killing fifty to eighty steelhead a year in the 1950s. As late as 1976 the yearly limit was set at forty steelhead!

Throughout the 1980s, sports anglers were allowed to kill up to ten steelhead each in the Bella Coola River, even though catch-and-release regulations had been widely imposed by then throughout British Columbia. For many during that time, the Bella Coola became the place to go because of its wide open fishery. And after making that long drive to the valley, many wanted to kill their limit to make their effort worthwhile.

Given all that happened, it's a wonder there are any Bella Coola steelhead left. How did the run hang on while the commercial fleet was eradicating the strongest fish at sea? How did any get past the wall of Native nets set near the mouth? How did any survive the onslaught of resident, nonresident, tourist and guided fishers all using roe and spinning gear and almost all killing every fish they caught?

And why didn't the government do something when there was a chance to? Why didn't managers see the excessive toll being taken by increased fishing, better fishing access and more efficient gear and techniques?

Even though steelhead have become mere ghosts in the river, there are still people in the valley who refuse to believe the fish are gone. Next year, they keep saying, the runs will be better. They believe the fish are out there somewhere and they will be back. Some still kill the fish they catch.

The Nuxalk call May Sinumwak, the Moon for Making Salmon Weirs. Historically, they took advantage of the low water, early in the month, to build salmon traps across bars and shallows that would soon be covered by spring floods. The remnants of the last of those weirs—perhaps the last one to function in North America—can be seen at Junction Pool, where the Atnarko and Talchako Rivers join to form the Bella Coola. Had that weir continued to operate, perhaps the walls of nets would never have existed—and the steelhead run might have survived.

Emerging from the forest near Burnt Bridge Creek, we begin to fish down along a riffle that is close to perfection for a fly caster. The current is steady. The water is just deep enough to provide ideal lies for the fish but shallow enough to enable any steelhead on the bottom to see a fly sweeping past overhead. We fish down in tandem—first me, with a dry line, then Harvey, with a sink tip. We make a cast or two, take a few steps and cast again. On one long swing, Harvey's fly stops, there is a great, stubborn weight, and then it comes undone.

"Maybe it was an early chinook," he says, because the fish was so solid, so unyielding.

With our Polaroid glasses we can look deep into the river. But we see nothing but shadowy stones and a few fry that dart for cover.

The survey crew said they saw fish holding here. And we can sense them. But the distance between us is immense.

Later we travel up the Atnarko, to a pool where thirty steelhead are said to be holding. Since 1966 this part of the river has been a no-fishing zone, so we walk the banks without our rods, hoping for a glimpse of one of the great fish.

All along the Bella Coola and up the Atnarko are old Nuxalk village sites. Their names give a rich sense of what they were. There is Snut'lh, Place of Dog Salmon; Nusats'm, Place of the Biggest Spring Salmon; and Asanani, Place Where Water Splash You. My favourite village name is N'Skeet, or Place Where You Screw a Woman. The story behind N'Skeet isn't talked about, but it is easy to romanticize, for in the meadows and along the forest edge grow a profusion of wildflowers: yellow heart-leaved arnica; white thimbleberry, saskatoon berry and star-flowered Solomon's seal; red western columbine and pink baldhip rose. There are twinflowers, greenish-white dogwood, wild sarsaparilla and mountain sweet cicely. Their scent is intoxicating, and the air vibrates with the buzz of pollinating insects.

The Nuxalk have long regarded the Atnarko as a sanctuary for salmon, and it is closed to all fishing because of that. A proposal to open it to dry fly-fishing for rainbow trout for one month a year was rejected by the government because of protests by the Nuxalk, who said they feared it would hurt chinook and steelhead. Paradoxically, the band at the time had dozens of lethal gill nets strung across the lower river, and they were indiscriminately killing the fish they said they wished to protect.

The Atnarko sanctuary is a languid, calm stretch of river, with one perfect holding pool after another. It is the kind of place you ache to cast a dry fly. There are logjams to shelter fish and deep cutbanks to hide under. One of the old Nuxalk sites here is known as Stwic, A Good Place to Rest, and looking at the river I realize it could be the home village of the steelhead.

All afternoon we walk along the Atnarko's banks, without seeing a steelhead. We see deer and lose track of the songbirds clamouring in the woods. There are concerns about a beetle infestation in the forest here, and some people have called for clear-cut logging to save the park. It seems to us, however, that the birds will take care of things in their own time. In the distance we hear the mystical, touching call of varied thrushes. The long, eerie, quavering whistled notes slowly fade away and then are repeated at a slightly higher pitch. It is haunting. The songs of the thrushes fall out of the dark green forest and echo off the still waters. Here and there, darting through openings in the woods, are Pacific flycatchers and wood warblers, which, like many of the other birds, time their return to the valley to coincide with the profuse insect hatches. Like steelhead, wood warblers migrate mostly at night.

We go up towards a pair of ramshackle cabins, remembering a story George Robson told about his fishing trips on the

Upper Atnarko. Starting in the 1930s he would come up every spring and stay with his father, Bert Robson, who pioneered here. They would fish in the river. In those days the pools were black with steelhead. There were also schools of whitefish, Dolly Varden and cutthroat. George said seven or eight steelhead would follow his lure on some casts. They would hook three or four in quick succession; then the steelhead would quit biting, so they'd move down to the next pool. The steelhead were dark by then, close to spawning, and didn't fight as well as the fresh fish in the lower river. But there were always fish here, he said. Always.

The best holding pool was located just downstream of Robson's, near the old cabin that belonged to Bert Matthew, another homesteader whose place has gone to ruin. There were so many steelhead—often two hundred or more in a school—that you could see ripples on the water as they shifted nervously about.

Robson said that with each passing decade he noticed there were fewer and fewer steelhead in the cabin pools. In the 1960s and 1970s you could still see thirty or more, but the trend was apparent. In 1993, fisheries biologists did a drift through the entire Upper Atnarko—and found only five steelhead. In one human generation the run had been destroyed.

We walk the banks, wondering what it must have been like and discussing ways the river can be restored. We say surely to God someone will do something about this. The government will declare a state of environmental emergency. They will stop the commercial and Native interceptions. They will put things right again. Surely. At the pool in which a fisheries surveyor counted thirty fish from a helicopter, I climb a rock to peer into the depths. Nothing.

We go up through an old meadow with waist-high grass standing dead from last fall. Then, coasting towards us, a shadow in the water. It wavers as it passes over a rift of golden sand and seems propelled by some hidden, inner energy source. There is no tail beat. And it is almost without form—merely a black elongated shape that, as we hold our breath, drifts into darkness and is gone. After that we stop to listen to the birds singing in the forest. There seems nothing else to do.

June

⌣

Spring Salmon Moon

The first chinook came in a small, clear stream on southern Vancouver Island, in a tidal pool so close to the ocean I could hear waves breaking on a nearby beach. How it was that a fish so huge could remain invisible until it rose from the bottom to take my fly is a mystery. Suddenly it was there, its enormous mouth gaping to engulf the bright orange fly. The hook was set in a tough piece of cartilage along the back rim of its black jaw. I braced for the fight. But the fish simply settled, dematerializing as its grey speckled back merged with the background colour of the river stones. All I could see was its pale shadow.

The trout rod was bent nearly double. I could feel where the fiberglass sank into the cork rings of the handle. I braced my right elbow against my lower ribs for support and grabbed the lower section of the rod with my left hand. We stayed locked like that, the fish unmoving. My arm soon ached. I didn't know what to do. No fish had ever acted like this before. It seemed indifferent to me. I tilted the rod to one side, changing the angle of tension, then snapped the tip up to provoke a run. But the fish didn't panic; it simply jerked its head to one side, pulling the rod towards the surface.

After a few minutes more I knew what I had to do. I wasn't equipped to fight a fish like this—nor did I want to kill such a magnificent salmon. I pointed the rod tip at him and pulled steadily on the line until the leader broke. The fish lay there, deep in the stream, the fly fluttering harmlessly in its jaw.

In June the Bella Coola River discolours with glacial silt and the water level rises to cover the exposed gravel bars. The rapids between the pools deepen and the biggest salmon of all move into the system. They are called spring salmon by some—because in many systems they arrive early in the year—or Tyee (Big Chief) when they pass the 30-pound (13.6-kilogram) mark. But most commonly they are known as chinook, a Salish name for the Chinook tribes of the lower Columbia River Valley and a Canadian term for a warm, moist southwest wind that blows from the sea.

Since that encounter on Vancouver Island, I have learned to fish for chinook with heavier gear. The fly rod is made of graphite, and the leader is short and strong, about 20-pound test. A line with a fast-sinking tip takes the fly down in the swift water. But all this and decades of experience are still no match for some of the chinook that swim in the Bella Coola, where the average weight is 9 kilograms and fish of 27 kilograms are not unheard of.

In most rivers in the Pacific Northwest, from Oregon to Alaska, chinook are in trouble. Populations have plummeted almost everywhere, largely because of overfishing by commercial fleets but also because of dams on the Columbia and widespread habitat degradation. As always, Native fishers and sports anglers have played their part, seeking out chinook above all other species—and killing the biggest. Sports fishing lodges, boasting some of the most skilled salmon guides in the world, have proliferated along the British Columbia coast because of the chinook runs, allowing anglers to get at the fish in places that before were far too remote.

On the Bella Coola, chinook runs fell dramatically—from 35,000 to fewer than 4500 chinook in 1979—but then rebounded to near historical levels after a federal government hatchery was opened, in 1981, to augment natural production. Target escapement (the number that return to spawn) for chinooks on the Bella Coola River system is 25,000 fish. During the early 1990s, thanks to the Snootli Creek Hatchery, the spawning escapement hit 28,000 fish. That run was miraculous, given the overall decline of chinook stocks, and it demonstrated what can be accomplished. About one-third of the returning fish were from the hatchery.

Although the runs were far below natural levels, they were strong enough to feed the public's increasing demand for salmon. Native, commercial and sports anglers have all clamoured for a bigger share of the catch. And the hatchery, in trying to meet that demand, unfortunately encouraged increased fishing. In the long run, wild stocks will decline unless the catch is reduced.

Typically, adult chinook appear near the mouth of the Bella Coola by the last week of April, and they begin their migration upstream shortly after. Peak migration takes place usually by the last week of June and is over by the end of July. The early run is followed by a second but relatively small wave of fish in August. The two runs are likely genetically distinct stocks, but studies haven't been done to verify that. By the end of August mature chinook have moved up through the Bella Coola and are holding in the deeper pools of the Atnarko River. They can be found throughout the lower Atnarko and may extend all the way to Knot Lake. Spawning is under way by the first week of September and ends in October. The main spawning areas are around Stuie and between Stillwater and the Hotnarko confluence. A few chinook spawn in the Salloomt River and up the Nusatsum River, but not many. The hatchery collects brood stock and uses its facilities to bump up natural production, a process that must be done carefully so that the river's wild gene pool isn't downgraded. Over the centuries, natural selection has produced a remarkable species of salmon in the Bella Coola.

Chinook usually spawn in the faster, deeper runs, where the force of water is simply too great for smaller species. They can successfully spawn in many conditions, however, if the gravel is adequate. Chinook don't feed after they've returned to the river, but they are aggressive fish, making them vulnerable to sports anglers. Nobody knows why chinook take a lure, but it appears they attack anything they judge a possible threat to their offspring. It's known that female chinook spend between four and twenty-five days defending their redds after spawning is completed. Surely this protective instinct must be in play before spawning takes place. Drift a fly—say, a big Muddler Minnow, which imitates an egg-eating sculpin—next to a chinook and watch the reaction. The salmon will turn to bite the fly and spit it out. It is not trying to eat it but intends to kill it. It is as if the salmon are trying to clean the river of threats to their eggs before they spawn in the weeks ahead.

In the Bella Coola, chinook fry begin to emerge by early April, peaking towards the end of the month and finishing by the third week of May. The outmigration of the fry almost immediately precedes the return of spawning chinook, and some scientists speculate that the smell of the outward-moving fry helps the adults locate their natal stream. Certainly the salmon use their olfactory powers to locate the plume of the Bella Coola and find their way back to the spawning grounds.

In the estuary, chinook fry grow quickly on a rich diet of chironomids, crab larvae, baby fish, sand fleas, daphnia, amphipods, juvenile herring, sticklebacks and other fish. As they grow they migrate farther down the inlet. Some stay in the inshore channels, while others range to the outside coast, where big breakers smash against the black shoreline and the sea is charged with energy. After a year or so, both types of chinook gradually move north to offshore feeding grounds in the Pacific Ocean and Bering Sea. As the salmon grow they become increasingly dependent on other fish for food, with herring making up 60 per cent of their diet. Fisheries managers say there is no link between the depletion of herring stocks and the overall decline of chinook populations, but many old sports anglers believe otherwise. Veteran British Columbia outdoors writers such as Mike Crammond and Lee Straight have pointed out, for example, that years ago, before the herring fishery reached insane proportions, chinook were heavier and obviously well fed. They also note that when herring vanish from an area, as they have done in many places on the coast, the chinook fishing soon collapses.

After three or four years feeding at sea, mature chinook, which have now grown from the length of your finger to the length of your arm, or longer, head in a more-or-less direct southeast line across the Pacific and back to their home rivers. Some chinook don't return until they have spent five or six years in the ocean, and typically these are the biggest fish of all—the giants that top 27 kilograms and that have reached 56 kilograms in some rivers. Few fly-fishers are equipped to land a chinook of over 13 to 18 kilograms, especially if it is a fresh fish that uses the force of the current to make its run. For this reason, searching the waters of the Bella Coola with a fly in June can be a daunting experience.

I rise early to look for chinook, slipping out into the cool dawn at just after 5:00 A.M. The timing is meant more to avoid other anglers than to correspond with the habits of the salmon, which can be seen in the river throughout the day when they rise to cleave the surface with their great, broad backs.

There's traffic on the highway. Commercial fishers are headed for the docks, their pickups laden with equipment. They acknowledge me as we pass in the way all early-morning commuters do in the Bella Coola Valley: with one finger raised from the steering wheel. It's a signal between those sharing the secret of dawn. They will have seen wildlife, heard the forest awakening and understood at some deep level that this is a time of rebirth.

Down on the waterfront boats are being readied for an opening that will come soon. In the 1950s and 1960s, May 24 was traditionally the start of chinook season for the fleet. There were 16 or 17 gill-net fishers from Bella Coola who would work the channel in those days. They would fish five days a week, for about seven or eight weeks—until the run was "played out." In the early 1950s they used linen nets but began switching to lighter, stronger nylon nets in 1954, and by 1957 everyone was using nylon.

George Robson, who was fishing the inlet in those days, said the new technology made the gill-netters a lot more efficient.

"What a difference. Boy, when the nylon nets first came out, they were killers compared with the linen nets," he said.

Spring salmon fishing was hard work. The fishers had to watch their nets closely because seals would get the fish, tearing them out of the webbing, leaving only a head behind. Sometimes seals would get caught themselves, ripping up and tangling a net as they thrashed about. The fishers occasionally hit a school of chinook, but usually the fish came a few at a time.

"The most Bella Coola chinook I ever got in a night of fishing was forty-one. Other guys did better," said Robson. "Glen MacKay got sixty one night and Don Egan got ninety. On the other hand, I once went three weeks, fifteen days of fishing and got no chinook! A lot of days we got none, then the next day one might get nine to twelve. In a good season I would get a couple hundred anyway. The largest chinook I ever caught was fifty-one pounds. Glen MacKay got a sixty-plus pounder once, and I heard of a few sixty-five-plus pounders caught over the years."

As more and more fishers began to fish Bella Coola chinook, fewer and fewer fish returned and it became harder for the Atnarko River to produce enough for the commercial harvest. The fishing days were cut back to four days a week, then three, then two, and by the late '90s they were down to one day a week for about four weeks.

Gill-netters, who take between two thousand and five thousand chinook each year, refer to chinook season now as a stamp fishery. To qualify for government unemployment payments, you need twelve weeks of fishing. Often a few weeks of chinook fishing is what makes the difference. Without unemployment payments, many commercial operators would go out of business. It's disturbing to think that chinook are required to carry such a load on their backs.

At least six user groups are killing wild Bella Coola chinook. Before the inshore gill-netters get a crack at them, the runs are hit by two outside troll fleets. Coded wire tag recoveries indicate that commercial trollers in southeastern Alaska take many Bella Coola chinook; Canadian commercial trollers also take them. A Native fishery on the lower Bella Coola takes nearly two thousand each year. And sports anglers kill between three hundred and eight hundred chinook annually in both the Bella Coola and upstream in the clear waters of the Atnarko, which is fished until July.

Heading down Salloomt Road I slow to cross a steel bridge over a rushing piece of water that broadens into a deep slot. There are already half a dozen spinning rods propped up along the riverbank, with a group of men standing around sipping coffee. They look up but give no sign of greeting. Behind them are four camper trucks. They have moved in for a few days or a week or two of chinook killing. When the river becomes closed to all but catch-and-release, anglers such as these will vanish from the valley, for they are interested in the Bella Coola only as long as they can kill the salmon they catch. I know that even if I stop here their fishing technique will make it impossible to fly-fish the run. They have staked out their water and will occupy it all day, every day. I could wait patiently for a turn, hoping one of them will reel in to clear some space, but I know it would be hopeless. They have gobs of roe sitting on the bottom, in the middle of the river, held in place by heavy weights. The anglers are waiting for a fish to swim past, take the roe and ring a little bell on the rod tip. At the bell, the anglers will scramble to grab the rod before it is pulled into the water. It could be hours or days before the little bell rings—and I know there have to be better places to fish.

Upstream a few hundred metres is the mouth of the Nusatsum River, where the water isn't as easy but where there is probably a chinook or two. It used to be a magnificent place to fish, before it was logged in the late 1950s and early 1960s. Before logging, the lower Nusatsum was a lazy creek that wound its way through a forest of giant spruce, cedar, hemlock and fir. There were deep pools, riffles and backwaters that provided protection and spawning sites for large fish all the way to the Highway 20 Bridge. Depending on the time of year, you could catch steelhead, coho, chinook or cutthroat there. But after the side hills were clear-cut the whole hydrology of the area changed. Streambanks eroded and pools filled in with silt. The lower Nusatsum became a straight chute, a sluice that rushed down to the Bella Coola River without pause.

Through the maze of nature you can easily trace a line from logging to the loss of salmon. The nourishing insect life is gone, the deep, sheltering pools are gone, the spawning gravel has vanished under layers of silt, and the juvenile fish that once inhabited the lower Nusatsum are almost all gone too.

In the decades since the area was logged, a healthy second-growth forest has grown back. It is the type of forest loggers point to to illustrate the temporary impact of their industry. But if you go through the forest and look into the river, you have to ask: What of the lost generations of salmon?

Walking down Nusatsum through a mixed coniferous-deciduous forest, with willow, alder and other thick shrubbery bordering the stream, I listen to the birds and hope some salmon have returned, to hold in the main river, below the mouth.

In the trills and arpeggio of bird song are a series of notes I haven't heard for almost a year, and I quietly detour off the trail. It sounds like an American robin, but the tone is shorter and hoarser. At the base of a large black cottonwood, looking up to the top branches, I spot a brilliant yellow, sparrow-sized bird, with black wings, black tail and a reddish-orange face. A pair of yellow wing bars flashes on the wings. The bird's dusky grey beak seems to be a cross between the slender pointed bill of a warbler and the massive conical bill of a grosbeak. It is a western tanager, back from his winter home in the tropical forests of Central America.

As I watch the brilliant bird, which looks as if it is made from smoke and compressed sunlight, the cascade of bird song falling from the canopy seems to grow louder. Vireos, thrushes, sparrows and woodwarblers are all singing, their notes ringing off each other and spinning into space. Surrounding me are skunk cabbages with giant leaves up to a metre long, patches of deer ferns that stand waist high and menacing thickets of towering devil's club, with leaves that are about half a metre wide and spiked stalks. The tanager, I realize, has traded a winter jungle for a summer one.

The Bella Coola River is high now, loud and greenish-grey-brown. Visibility is down to less than half a metre. Spring runoff from the Interior Plateau and surrounding mountains has begun to subside, but instead of becoming clearer and less brown, the river has turned dark as glacial flour pours in from the Talchako, Nooklikonnik and Nusatsum Rivers. The freezing level has risen above the tree line, and the streams from the glaciers are flowing.

The high, dirty water suits the large chinook just fine. Because of their enormous strength, they have no difficulty moving up against the current and seem to appreciate the cover the silt provides. Periodically they surface, as if to view their surroundings. Some anglers believe the fish are really "tasting" the surface water—and maybe there is something to that, because they are using their powerful sense of smell to search for their spawning grounds.

Across the stream are rock bluffs. Hidden beneath the high-water mark are petroglyphs that emerge, like the faces of the seasons, when the river drops. Standing along the far bank is a grove of Douglas fir, hemlock and spruce. You can walk there on bear trails worn into the dark earth and listen to the drowsy *wee-wee-wee* songs of Townsend's warblers, birds that are dependent on old growth. There are places near here where human skulls and bone fragments glint, far back in the closed darkness of rock crevices. These are not burial caves but places of last refuge, where Nuxalk went alone to die during a smallpox outbreak nearly a century ago. They had come out of the forest and they went back to it. The sunlight comes through in spectral shafts of gold, and high above, the wind brushes the canopy. Sometimes you think there are voices whispering, and maybe there are.

There was once a Nuxalk village near here known as Nusatsum—Place of the Biggest Spring Salmon. Some chinook still run up the milky Nusatsum River, but not many, and no one has really noticed that the fish are particularly big. Native stories, however, even when steeped in myth, have a remarkable degree of truth to them. I would bet there once was a giant Nusatsum chinook that may have been wiped out by nets—or by the logging that destroyed so much of the nursery water on the lower river.

Along the water's edge a spotted sandpiper moves nervously, its tail bobbing up and down and its head rocking forward towards the ground as it runs across the bar. Its belly is white, its back olive-brown, and round, black spots are splattered everywhere. The bird looks as if it is made from sand and gravel. It utters a shrill *peet-weet* several times, then quickly flies away upstream. I know its mate must be somewhere near, perhaps huddled on an invisible nest.

As I string my rod I watch the slick waters at the tail of the pool. If a fresh salmon moves in, it will likely roll here and may hold for a time across the fan of gravel. The current will sweep the fly up and across the shallows, and by mending my line I will be able to swing it past the face of a waiting salmon—if I know just where the fish is lying. It is impossible to see the bottom through the glacial silt. So I wait. After fifteen minutes, the back of what looks to be a 9-kilogram chinook humps above the surface. It is a fresh fish, dark greenish-blue, with shiny silver sides. I mark the spot.

Wading into the river, my feet feeling carefully across the slick stones, I check the reel tension, pull hard on the knots to make sure they are secure and test the sharpness of the hook, pricking the end of my thumb. The barb has been filed off.

The leader is only about a metre long. Even in clear water, salmon aren't line shy, and in the silted Bella Coola, the dark heavy fly line won't bother them. The fly is a large, black leech pattern. There aren't any leeches in the river, but the strip of black rabbit fur is highly visible and it undulates in a way that annoys chinook. When they take it, it is usually with a savage strike. The leader is 20-pound test.

The first dozen casts swing across the tail of the pool untouched, passing over the place where I think the salmon lies. It is a tense business, fishing blind but knowing a great salmon is there, somewhere. I am on the line, ready for any touch. I see the fish take the fly before I feel it, as the line hesitates, and the fish strikes into a huge surface swirl. Immediately I feel the unmistakable heaviness of a chinook shaking its powerful head. Then the fish bolts, turning into the current and running downstream. I stumble out of the water, running along the bar and startling a second sandpiper, which rises from among the rocks, frantically calling. I lean on the rod and try to turn the fish but cannot. I throw out slack, letting it belly in the current, so the salmon feels pressure from downstream—the fish pauses for a moment, but as I run closer it charges away again. The fly line whips off the reel, followed by nearly 200 metres of backing. The fish feels much bigger than 9 kilograms, but it doesn't jump and I can't see it. The line vanishes into the water. With all my backing gone and the fish outrunning me, I drop the rod tip, signalling defeat, and lock the reel by grabbing the spinning spool with my right hand. For a brief, shocking moment, the full weight of the salmon comes against me—the rod, the line and the river all buck together. Then the line parts. I reel in to find the fly broken off at the tip.

Shaken, I walk back upstream, only to see another chinook roll in the tailout, precisely where I'd marked the first fish. This time I cast from below, hoping that when the fish takes it, it will run upstream, against the current. It takes on the third cast, its tail partially clearing the surface as it wallows over on the fly. It quarters out into the fast current but then turns in towards the deeper, slower water. It runs to the head of the pool, hits the current, turns back, jumps, opening an enormous hole in the surface, and makes two more long runs before it begins to tire. Arms shaking, I finally draw it alongside. It is under 13 or 14 kilograms, but not by much, and it was all the fish I could handle. It rests against my knees, as I work the hook loose. Big glaring eyes, silver cheeks, pectoral fins that look the size of my hands. With the hook out of the fish's tough jaw, the current presses the fish against my legs. I reach over, plunging my arm elbow deep, soaking my coat, to cradle the fish for a moment. It gulps water steadily, silt streaming in over the gills and trailing off its scales, and then with a tail beat that thumps against me, it pushes off and is gone.

July

Sockeye Salmon Moon

Harvey and I zip up on the side of the road. The neoprene sailboarding suits soon make us sweat. Heat waves rise from the pavement, and the forest buzzes and cracks around us. The birds, now too busy feeding young to worry about territorial declaratives or expressions of sexual yearning, have grown silent. Wading boots on, masks and snorkels in hand, we plunge into the green woods, desperate for shade. It's about a kilometre to the Atnarko, which lies somewhere below us, down a steep bank and across tableland that is perfect grizzly habitat. Along the way we pass a little kettle pond formed by the melting of ice blocks buried in the outwash fan of a huge retreating glacier. Pure seepage water is cupped in a bowl of clay hardpan. Pond lilies grow along the shallow shoreline, and farther out patches of green algae cling to submerged branches. We see stocked, 35-centimetre cutthroat trout cruising languidly, occasionally rising to take caddis flies that teasingly settle on the water to lay eggs.

Sparkling blue-and-green dragonflies shoot past, in pursuit of mosquitoes, and a cedar waxwing drops from a branch to take one of the big insects in midflight.

In July (Silhcwm), the Bella Coola system is rapidly filling with salmon now. Chinook and a handful of steelhead are in holding lies, while the sockeye have just started running in strength. The earliest of the pink, coho and chum are arriving too. Despite the difficulties many of the salmon runs are in, there is a sense of richness to the river in the summer, as all the salmon tribes begin to gather. For a short time the river seems as it once was—as all West Coast salmon rivers once were.

It is believed all Pacific salmon evolved from a common ancestor that thrived in the ocean 100 million years ago. The life cycle of the primitive fish was probably much like that of modern salmon and sea-run trout. Spawning took place in fresh water, where there was less predation than in the sea, and maturity was achieved in the food-rich oceans. Over great time, different salmon species evolved—but they all continued to follow the same strategy.

It is an axiom that no two species can occupy the same ecological niche indefinitely. So how is it that all the salmon species can survive in a common river? The answer lies in the subtle ways the species have evolved to divide the waters among themselves. The result is that the available freshwater habitat produces far more biomass than it would if only one species spawned in the system. Because they have evolved to use microhabitats, the ancient salmon have been enormously successful, despite natural disasters, environmental changes and the onslaught of commercial fishing.

Salmon species are different in size and appearance; they differ in the water depths and stream velocities they use for spawning and rearing their young; and they have differences in eating habits and in preferred food organisms; differences in how long they reside in fresh water and salt water; differences in the timing of spawning and in their migrations. Some of the differences are obvious, some not. These variations on a theme keep the species ecologically isolated from one another in space and/or time. The fly-fisher instinctively knows that each species has its own preferred stream location and, through trial and error and keen observation, soon learns where to fish. But when you swim a river, using a face mask to peer beneath the reflective surface, you see the separations even more clearly—and it is startling to learn how wrong you can be assessing water from above. Runs you'd think would be empty hold lots of fish—and seemingly perfect pools are often barren.

As we tramp through the woods, mosquitoes buzz around our heads, attracted by our body heat and our trail of carbon dioxide. We stop to spray on bug dope, but it soon comes off with our sweat. Finally the river is just below, and we slide down pine needles coating a steep bank to splash into the water. The Atnarko is clear and sparkling, and it tugs at my legs as I wash the face mask, pull it on and lift my feet to be swept away. I catch my breath, as much from the shock of changing worlds as from the surge of coldness.

Swimming a river is a lot like drifting one in a boat. You stay to the inside edge on bends, where the water is slower, and keep an eye out for shallow rocks and trees that lean out from the bank, known as sweepers. You go head first, swimming slightly faster than the current. In rapids you keep your hands out in front of you, body slightly bowed, like a whitewater canoe. You are so buoyant that you slide over most boulders.

It seems easy, and you feel graceful and soaring as you slip down a quick glide, the gravel bed flashing with sunlight below you. Then you try to stop, catching a rock and swinging around —and the current suddenly crashes into you. It is driving, irresistible, as if the force of gravity has pivoted sideways. The human body, it quickly becomes evident, is anything but streamlined; it is blocky and cumbersome and weak. The fish, by contrast, hang effortlessly in the current, as the water sluices around their smooth bodies.

After a fast run, surrounded by blinding white air bubbles and the roar of water, I fall over the lip of the rapids and into the silence of a deep pool. My body settles and I can feel the temperature change from cool to hard coldness as I drift into the shadow of the forest. Gradually giving way below me is a small group of big, dark-bodied chinook, six fish that sink deeper and drift backwards. They feel hidden in the shadow of a rock shelf and let me draw close. I see a gold rim in their eyes. Then they bolt past with a few swipes of their tails and vanish. Their acceleration is miraculous.

In the riffles and fast-running glides of the Atnarko we see juvenile steelhead darting after insects, pine needles and anything else that looks like a meal. Juvenile chinook are found in slightly slower water and are more likely to be along the margins of the deeper pools. There are no pink or chum fry evident, which is expected, because they migrate downstream shortly after hatching to rear in the estuary. We see few cutthroat or coho fry—most are still in small tributary streams, beaver ponds or sloughs along the Bella Coola.

When you swim into a pool you sometimes see several species of mature salmon mingling as they manoeuvre to let you past. But if you hold at the tailout for a moment and give them time to settle, they soon separate into their own groupings again.

Holding in a pool below fast water, the salmon often cycle up to the lip of the rapid and then drop back, as if judging the force of the current before they decide to run it—much the way a kayaker might.

The difference between the underwater world and our own is profound, dramatic and as thin as the surface layer. At Belarko Pool, where the light plays beautifully over the river stones and salmon hold like kites in the current, I lift my head just a few centimetres—and hear laughter and excited screams. Several people sit on the gravel bar in colourful lawn chairs while their kids splash in the shallows. The sounds and colours seem harsh and unreal, and they vanish as I drop my face again into the Atnarko. Hanging listless, drifting where the current takes me, I lose touch with my body and start to melt into the green light. Only the sound of my lungs brings me back.

Just below Belarko Pool the river divides. One branch goes to the left; the other continues straight ahead. Deep in the water, eerily out of place, there's a pair of sweatpants caught on a snag, flapping in the current. Scattered across the bottom are the shattered remains of a drift boat, an uncomfortable reminder of the power of the river. Just a few weeks earlier four anglers tried to run this channel. Their boat smashed into a large sweeper, flipped under the log and became jammed between a hard place and an unforgiving force of nature. Three of the anglers managed to jump to safety, but the fourth was swept downstream, flailing against the current. He was hurled against a logjam—and sucked under. His pants and one shoe got hung up but were ripped from his body. He swallowed water, suffered cuts, bruises and broken ribs, and may have said his prayers, but amazingly he found his way through the dark logjam, surfaced and survived. My throat feels dry and I look up cautiously. The twilight of the logjam, which lies down the run ahead, is not something I want to experience.

With a few strong strokes, I veer down the left branch, headed for open water and Bear Hole. On the cliffs above are tree trunks that have been rubbed smooth by the backs of bears. Coarse ginger and black hair sticks in the pitch, and expanded footprints, where generations of bears have carefully stepped in each other's tracks, mark the forest floor. Nobody knows why bears behave this way, like religious zealots approaching a shrine in a prescribed, ritualistic manner. At rubbing trees and only at rubbing trees, bears walk in the paw prints of those who have gone before them. The effect is to create what looks like the footprints of a dinosaur as each bear widens and deepens the tracks. It is mystical, unsettling.

Along the margins of the pool, where the depths shine with sunlight like stained glass in a church, I slow to watch a flaring school of chinook fry. As I approach, crawling into the shallows, they hide under stones, burrowing from sight. Within minutes they come out again and begin to forage. After hatching, both chinook and steelhead inhabit river margins, where they are eaten by kingfishers, mergansers and other predators. The tiny fish are fast to react but are no match for the lightning stab of a beak or claw. Only the quick survive. As the juvenile fish grow larger, they move away to deeper water, where their size and strength is crucial in evading larger fish. Hatchery salmon and trout, which are often raised to the smolt stage in sheltered tanks, are stupendously inept at fleeing to safety. Some hatchery managers have wondered if cutthroat trout should be set among the penned fry, to teach them how to flee and to weed out the weak.

Below Bear Pool the river runs west again down to Steelhead Run. In the greenish-blue water I search for the distinctive, square-tailed outline of a steelhead but see none. A school of large mountain whitefish huddles near the middle of the pool in monastic silence.

Below Steelhead Run the Atnarko makes a gentle turn northwards, along Eagle's Nest Run and down to the Corner Pool— probably the deepest pool I will pass through. As I slowly drift over the blackness, I watch thick-bodied chinook of up to 22 or 23 kilograms sink away from me. The chinook drop towards the tailout and then dart past me to the sanctuary of dark water. After spending years out in the vast greenness of the ocean, the large fish must feel exposed and vulnerable in the confined river. Or do they, returning after all these years, recognize this as home?

Glinting softly amid the stones on the bottom of the pool is an amazing array of lead weights. Strewn here and elsewhere in the river are thousands of weights lost by anglers whose lines broke off on fish or on underwater snags. Could all this lead have an impact on the fish, birds or even people of the Bella Coola Valley?

The shifting rocky bottom of the stream must grind some of the lead into little bits that probably find their way into the food web. True, the volume of flowing water is enormous, but like DDT, lead concentrates in living organisms by a process of bioaccumulation. A study reviewing 12,000 bird mortalities in British Columbia found that 247 suffered lead poisoning. Most were water birds or raptors. In another study, researchers estimated that over fifty years nearly 10,000 swans from fourteen countries died from poisoning caused by lead fishing weights, shotgun pellets or contamination from mining and smelting wastes. Lead shot has been widely banned. Perhaps it's time to do the same with lead fishing weights.

Below Corner Pool the Atnarko River turns west again at the Wagon Wheel Run and then flows down through the upper Corbould's Bridge area. At one time the Wagon Wheel was among the most productive steelhead runs on the river, a legendary pool that anglers approached with excited anticipation. But not anymore. I see a school of bright silver sockeye, some whitefish, a few small rainbow trout and a pair of chinook seeking cover on the downstream side of a submerged log. There are no steelhead.

The road from Corbould's Bridge leads up to Tweedsmuir Lodge, one of the most famous old lodges on the coast, though it has fallen into obscurity in recent years. Tweedsmuir was the home of the late Tommy Walker, an Englishman who emigrated to the Bella Coola Valley in 1929. He arrived by steamship and made his way 60 kilometres up a narrow twisting gravel road to find that the lodge he'd bought was an unfinished log cabin. He cleared land for a farm, helped build and operate Stuie (later renamed Tweedsmuir) Lodge and became a professional guide and outfitter. He sold the lodge to Colonel Corbould around 1948 and then left to explore the Spatsizi Wilderness. Using his connections and his persuasive command of language, Walker, more than anyone else, is responsible for the establishment of Tweedsmuir Park, which, since 1937, has protected the Bella Coola's headwaters.

Walker was also one of the first fly-fishers on the Bella Coola River. He must have seemed an odd character in those rough-and-tumble days. Few anglers were interested in sports fishing then, and fewer still ever released a fish alive. In his book Spatsizi, Walker recalls his first fishing experience in the valley, when an acquaintance showed him the local angling technique—throwing a stick of dynamite into a pool.

During his time at Tweedsmuir Lodge, Walker developed a regular clientele of fly-fishers and established a world-class sports fishery for Bella Coola steelhead. His work paved the way for the many guides who followed in his footsteps—Stener Saugstad, Lloyd Brynildsen, Al Elsey, Ken Stranaghan, Dick Blewett, Rob Stewart, Les Kouluk and others.

Just below Corbould's Bridge, the river turns again to flow in a northwesterly direction. At the end of a 600-metre run is a well-known pool called the Swimming Hole, or the Ulkatcho Net Site, because it is where the Anahim people net sockeye. There are no nets today, just teenaged kids swinging on ropes and dropping down into the water with a deep, soft, plooshing sound.

Through rapids below, bullied by the current and bouncing off a rock or two, I eventually tumble into the Smokehouse Pool, which is deep and turbulent. Grabbing a large boulder, I cling to it in the frothy water. The fast water is often the best place to look for large resident rainbow trout.

In the chaos of the tumbling water it takes a moment to get oriented. But soon I start seeing fish. Below me and to each side, ghosting in and out of the foam, is a pack of a dozen rainbow trout. Most are under 15 centimetres but two of them are much larger. One is close to 2 kilograms, the other a bit smaller. Neither seems threatened by my presence.

Bella Coola rainbows are beautiful fish, heavily spotted on their dorsal fins and over their backs, with a bold red stripe along each side. The fish strategically place themselves just on the edge of the main current, lying with their heads upstream and tilted slightly upwards. Sliding back and forth in the current and showing perfect body-fin-eye coordination, the fish periodically change position to gracefully intercept aquatic insects. At times a small fish darts to the surface and snaps a floating bit of wood or a conifer needle. My rough ride through the shallow rapids above has dislodged aquatic insects, silt and debris, and the fish are taking advantage of it. When the big fish feed, they rise smoothly to the surface, take a fly by tipping up, and settle again, with little exertion. The juveniles move rapidly, frequently taking items that aren't edible and spitting them out.

There are, of course, advantages to being the first to gobble up drifting debris, even if much of it is inedible. Studies have shown that food, not space, limits juvenile survival in the summer. The fish that grab the most food are the ones that grow larger.

A few fish search the bottom for insects, while others surface to feed or to swallow air to refill their swim bladders. Fish are naturally heavier than water and require the use of internal air bladders to help regulate their position under water. When the air in the bladder needs to be replenished, all salmon must come to the surface—a practice that sometimes reveals the holding lies of big steelhead, chinook and other nonfeeders that might otherwise stay hidden.

Watching fish under water is a wonderful way to gain an appreciation for how well adapted they are and how they position themselves in the river. Their bodies, senses and behaviour combine to make them extremely efficient predators. All have a streamlined, torpedo shape that helps move them rapidly through the water aided by a series of muscles that power a broad tail. As a general rule, most salmon can reach speeds of ten times their body length per second. Adult steelhead, which cruise for days at 1.4 metres per second, can accelerate to 8 metres per second (darting speed). Salmon and steelhead can jump up to 3 metres in the air, perhaps higher, provided they begin their vault in a deep pool.

Salmon and trout have a well-developed sense of vision, but they are shortsighted. That's why they sometimes come to within centimetres of a fly before turning away in refusal. They can see objects 3 to 4.5 metres away, but not as clearly as a human would. Although salmon may not see as far as humans, they do have a much larger area of peripheral vision because their eyes are located on the sides of the head and they move independently. Fish can look forwards, laterally, backwards, downwards and straight ahead. Like humans, fish see colour (blue, green and red), and they are able to see at low levels of light (starlight). Although fish may not be able to sharply see the silhouette of a fisher in their peripheral vision, they readily detect movement against a contrasting background.

Unlike the pupil of the human eye, the pupil of a fish does not react quickly to changes in light conditions. It can take up to two hours for a fish to adapt fully to a change from bright to dark conditions. This phenomenon may explain why fish often stop feeding immediately after dusk.

Studies show that salmon and trout can taste and feel the objects in their mouths. This is probably why hard flies and those made of plastic or enamelled materials are almost always ejected immediately after the fish have mouthed them. Flies constructed of soft materials (feathers, furs or soft synthetics) are often held much longer—giving the angler more time to set the hook.

Although trout and salmon do not hear in the same sense that humans do, they can detect sound vibrations (pressure waves) travelling through the water from more than 9 metres away. So they can easily sense you wading, in still water. The sound vibrations are detected by otolithic structures in an inner ear and by special sensors located in the lateral line of the fish. Fish can actually determine the size, direction and speed of moving objects. A fish's sense of "hearing" is so sensitive that it can detect wriggling fish or worms a few metres away. The lateral line is also used to monitor water temperature, variations in currents and depths.

In addition to such powerful senses, salmon have other abilities that are not yet understood. Although it is known that they use visual clues and their sense of smell to find their spawning streams, there are other mysterious factors at work. In one scientific experiment, salmon that had been blinded were able to find their spawning grounds. So were fish that had their sense of smell removed. Amazingly enough, a small percentage of fish that could neither see nor smell also managed to find their way home.

Most fly-fishers quickly learn that few salmon and trout tolerate clumsy wading or sloppy casts that slap the surface. They try to approach a stream carefully and learn to use swift, flowing riffles as cover. Fish that are unaware of your presence are more easily tempted into taking a fly.

I feel comfortable in the white water at Smokehouse Pool, tucked in behind a sheltering boulder. But when I let go the current tumbles me over, blinding me with foam, until I am swept into calmer water. At the tailout, the white bellies of several dead rainbow trout shine up at me from the bottom. They had been caught and released, I knew, by anglers who had been fishing here with roe for chinook. I wonder what the total kill is on the river. In a season it must number into the hundreds.

The Atnarko flows in a gentle southwesterly direction below the Smokehouse Pool for about 400 metres and then curves back towards Fisheries Pool, passing through Woodpecker Run, Gooseberry Run, Sourdough Pool and Siwash Hill Run along the way. In some of them I see the gossamer-white, glinting reflections of fishing lines, drawn tight by weights on the bottom. The kill fishery for chinook is over now, however, and relatively few anglers are on the river.

Sockeye are shouldering into many of the pools, but here, as in most rivers in British Columbia, sports fishing for the red salmon is forbidden. The reason for not having a sports sockeye fishery has more to do with politics than conservation. Sockeye have always been the favourite target of the commercial salmon industry. The fish are easy to catch, particularly in seine nets, because the runs return over a short period of time and become concentrated in large numbers. In confined places, such as Johnstone Strait, near Campbell River on Vancouver Island, the seine fleet can take one million sockeye in a single twenty-four-hour opening.

Sockeye tend to be a uniform size, typically about 3 kilograms, which makes them relatively easy to process in large numbers. The flesh of sockeye is firm, has a good flavour and a high oil content, and is an attractive orange-red. Sockeye have always been a favourite food fish on the West Coast. The earliest canning operations in the Pacific Northwest were established primarily to exploit sockeye. Sockeye canneries were being built along the Fraser and Skeena in the 1870s, were established at Rivers Inlet in the 1880s and were on the Bella Coola by the early 1900s. Although many of the canneries have since shut down, victims of industrial centralization, millions of sockeye continue to be processed yearly. The killing of sockeye is big business.

For years, to protect their own interests, commercial fishers and fish processors successfully lobbied government to ban recreational fishers from keeping sockeye. But times are changing. After years of pressure from recreational anglers, the government has begun opening a few rivers to limited sockeye sports fisheries. More will have to follow.

Although a handful of sports anglers have long known that sockeye would readily take a lure at sea, few were aware until relatively recently that they could also be taken in fresh water. Experimental sports fisheries for sockeye were allowed in the Fraser and Skeena Rivers in 1996—and the results were astonishing. Not only would sockeye take an assortment of lures, but they would take flies more readily than just about any other species. Some anglers on the Fraser reported taking forty-five salmon a day on hot, lime-green flies fished over shallow bars.

Among the most effective sockeye salmon flies are those that are small (#6, 8 or 10), sparsely dressed and scarlet or chartreuse. Bright silver sockeye salmon take flies in many ways. Some anglers report "a jolting, well-pronounced strike," and others describe it as a "soft, subtle take—like a trout on a dead-drifted nymph."

The Bella Coola system, and particularly the Atnarko, would probably support a remarkable sockeye sports fishery. The salmon come in so quickly from the sea that they are still bright silver and green by the time they reach the Atnarko. And they are aggressive fish.

After a little more than an hour swimming down the Atnarko, I emerge, tired, bruised and numb from the cold. But I know the sockeye are in, and I will be back to try for them—after the river has been given time to shift the salmon within it and remake the mystery. Our drift has given us a deep appreciation of how currents work and has shown us precisely where the fish are holding. But an angler is meant to read a river by sight and by sound and to trust to luck. We have no desire to start casting now to the fish we have just swum with.

A few days later we return with fly rods to fish by instinct. On a warm day, with the yellow-centred ox-eye daisies nodding in a gentle breeze and white cabbage butterflies lilting over the fields, we dress for summer fishing: wading boots, shorts, T-shirt and nothing more.

Using a sinking line, 3-foot leader and sparsely dressed silver-and-lime-green fly, I cast across the Atnarko and let the current take the offering in a wide sweep across the pool. Surprisingly, I hook several steelhead smolts in a row, releasing them as quickly and as carefully as I can—and thinking of the white bellies I'd seen on the bottom earlier.

The young steelhead are voracious, and it is difficult to keep them off the fly, which matches a green inchworm falling from riverside trees. Steelhead are among the last of the salmon species to smolt, and these were just preparing to head out to sea. I didn't want to interrupt the journey. Switching to a chartreuse fly, I find a pattern the small steelhead don't seem to like and manage to sink it to where the sockeye should be holding. On the fifth cast there is a gentle take and I set the hook tentatively, not knowing what to expect. When the weight of the rod goes home there is an explosive run, then a short, powerful fight. A sockeye of about 2 kilograms comes in, its back greenish-blue, its flanks flashing silver. It is fresh from the sea and I can't tell whether it's a female or male. In a few weeks, the sockeye will undergo dramatic changes. Its body will turn brick-red and its head will become moss-green. The males will develop pronounced humps near the dorsal fin and their jaws will become deeply hooked, with protruding canine teeth. But for the moment, this fish is all white and silver and shaped like a torpedo—a perfect sports fish, beautiful and strong and willing to take a fly. I slip it back into the water, wishing I could keep it.

The Bella Coola sockeye stocks are not as healthy as they appear at first glance, and if a sports fishery is developed, as it should be, to allow more people to experience these salmon, the run will first have to be restored, or at-sea interceptions will have to be reduced.

Target escapement to the Atnarko is 75,000 sockeye. The average escapement has been around 39,000 fish, however, with highs of 150,000 and lows of 7500. Historically Bella Coola sockeye supported both an important commercial fishery and several commercial canneries. But since about 1990 the Bella Coola sockeye run has been depressed to the point that the commercial fleet has not been allowed to target sockeye after they move into Burke Channel. The closure was a major blow to the local commercial fishers. For many years sockeye were the fish that Bella Coola gill-netters depended on for their living. Sockeye season usually started the last Sunday in June and lasted until around July 18. Then the gill-netters would switch to pink salmon.

Native people are still allowed to net sockeye salmon, and of course the commercial fleet takes them outside the Burke Channel area. The Bella Coola Native food fishery begins in June, and the Ulgatcho from Anahim Lake also come down to fish just before haying season. Collectively the Nuxalk and Ulgatcho food fisheries take about five thousand sockeye annually.

Increasing pressure on the run, however, is being felt because the Bella Bella community, located on the outer coastal islands, is turning to Bella Coola stock. The Bella Bella's traditional sockeye run was on the Koeye River. But overfishing by Native seine boats and the commercial non-Native fleet helped cause the collapse of Koeye River sockeye stocks.

After that Bella Bella Native seiners began catching Rivers Inlet sockeye until the Owikeeno-Kitisu Tribal Council complained and forced them out. To fulfil their food fishery demands, the Bella Bella then turned to Bella Coola and Kimsquit Lake sockeye. The impact is not yet clear, but it is an ominous development.

We fish through the heat of the afternoon and into the early evening, catching and releasing sockeye and hoping that one of the 2-kilogram resident rainbows might take. The river seems like a perfect place—and we know the fishing is going to get better. Soon the pinks and chum will arrive in full force.

August

Dog Salmon Moon

Early August and magic falls from the skies. To the northeast, over the dark bulk of Four Mile Mountain, meteors radiate from the Perseus constellation to shower across the heavens. To the south, over brooding Mount Fougner, where the forest has been stripped in great clear-cuts, there are more streaks of orange and yellow left by meteorites emanating from Aquarius. When the Perseids fall, sometimes as many as seventy flashes of light an hour can be counted as the chunks of ice and stone strike the atmosphere, leaving shimmering trails. On a dark, clear, windless night you can see meteors reflecting from the surface of the sea, and sometimes it seems as if they are streaking through the ocean itself.

One still night I looked into the water and saw Polaris, hanging brightly off the lip end of the Big Dipper, pointing the way north. Birds are known to use the stars during migration, and scientists say salmon may do the same thing. Certainly they seem in tune with the heavens as they navigate home from the vastness of the North Pacific to find the narrow slot where Bentinck Arm opens a path through the mountains to the broad estuary of the Bella Coola River. As the Perseids arrive the biggest salmon migration of the year comes in, as hundreds of thousands, sometimes millions, of pinks and chum return. The two species travel separately but converge on the river mouth, like meteor showers coming from their own corners of the universe.

The stiff grass rasps against my waders as I make my way across the meadow towards the tidal flats. Sea gulls cry in the distance, their high, sharp calls carried by the wind. Twice a day the sea withdraws from the estuary exposing an expanse of rich, dark mud, where the birds feed. When it floods back in, salmon fry and other small fish come with it, rollicking in a rich soup of tiny organisms stirred up by the leading edge of water.

Low tide is the best time to learn an estuary. When the water drops you can locate deadheads, stumps and deep slots cut by currents coursing over the flats. At midtide many of those obstacles have vanished and the estuary has taken on a uniform look. The best time for fishing an estuary is three hours before high tide until perhaps an hour after, as the fish ride in with the rising waters. If you are lucky, you will see a school of sea-run cutthroat, swirling on the surface in pursuit of tiny fish. Sometimes you will cast to a disturbance like that—and a salmon will take, surprising you with a sudden, violent run.

Early morning or late evening offers the best conditions because of the stiff westerly winds that come blustering down North Bentinck Arm. The wind rises during late morning and often blows until sundown, making fly casting almost impossible. Cutthroat beach fishing is rarely productive in the Bella Coola estuary, perhaps because I don't yet know enough, but the estuary is a fascinating place that is full of promise and it keeps drawing me back. And in August, when the heavens are at their brightest, the chance of hitting a salmon increases dramatically.

Unlike most major salmon streams on the Pacific coast, the Bella Coola estuary is remarkably pristine. It is one of the few undeveloped major estuaries left from California to Alaska. And it was almost destroyed.

There are wharves and net sheds down the inlet on the southern shore, but the great sweep of the estuary itself, where the river braids into half a dozen channels to pass through grassy flats, is virtually untouched. Here and there are parts of old fishing boats, log dump pilings and the rusted relics of steam donkey hulks. But permanent industrial development has never taken place because of the rapid silt buildup, the tides, the periodic seasonal floods and the stubborn will of the local people.

That the Bella Coola River estuary will remain pristine is largely because of the foresight of the Nuxalk and in particular that of elder Art Saunders. In 1991, Saunders sold 47.8 hectares on the north side of the Bella Coola River to the Pacific Estuary Conservation Program. By locking it away, he virtually ensured that the estuary would be safe forever. The mandate of the Pacific Estuary Conservation program is to acquire, protect, enhance and manage wetland habitat in perpetuity. The land was a prime development site and Saunders could have sold it for a lot more, but he said he wanted "to give it to the ducks and salmon."

Earlier, in the 1970s, the Nuxalk as a community made a momentous decision about the estuary when a Japanese company tried to develop a pulp mill there. Pulp mill representatives spent large sums of money to try to convince the Nuxalk to agree to the development. There were promises of jobs for 100 to 130 people a day and instant wealth for the Nuxalk. In a final attempt to convince the band council and Nuxalk elders, the company took the group to Washington State to observe one of the company's most modern mills. Things were going well until a Nuxalk councillor asked a pointed question. As they watched waste water pouring out of the mill's effluent treatment system, the councillor asked a company representative, "Would you drink that water?" He replied, no, and so did the Nuxalk.

The Ojibwa in northern Ontario accepted when a similar proposal was made to them in the 1970s. But the Wabigoon-English River system was later closed to fishing when studies revealed that local residents had accumulated high levels of mercury in their blood. With their economy drastically changed and traditional pursuits curtailed, social problems soon plagued the community.

If the Nuxalk had agreed to the pulp mill, the inshore winds that blow down the inlet would have bathed their community in smoke carrying sulfides and mercaptans, and the estuary would have become laced with dioxins, furans, organochlorines and other chemicals that collect in sediment, plants, birds and fish. Today the wind blowing down Bentinck Arm carries only the smell and the sound of the sea.

The best way to get to the estuary is to cross an old overgrown meadow just west of the Bella Coola townsite and then to make your way through the mud flats a few hundred metres to the river. Crab apple trees, alders and shrubs such as Nootka rose have sprung up in the grassy field that once served as an airstrip.

All around me I hear the snapping of lupine pods releasing seeds in the warm summer sun. The peak season for flowers has long past, but at the tips of some of the plants are remnant blossoms. I stoop to catch the fragrance. Several ladybugs scurry for shelter on the leaves where they have been hunting for aphids.

I have trouble walking across the meadow because the grass is so thick and high. Just a few months ago it was ankle level, but in the rich soil, away from shade trees, the grasses have flourished. Clouds of insects rise with each step: leafhoppers, moths and adult spittlebugs skitter ahead of me.

From a sweet gale thicket come the calls of a common yellowthroat and a song sparrow, both insect eaters that feed in the meadow. On the branches of large spruce trees bordering the estuary, bald eagles have begun to congregate. Their guano stains the trunks, and feathers litter the ground in places. After I pass through a dense patch of dead willows, killed by borer beetles, the estuary opens before me. There are no more trees, just grasses, sedges and a variety of perennial forbs. From here down, tides cover the plants for at least part of the day. This area of the Bella Coola estuary is called the intertidal zone, and the ground gets softer underfoot. Here the plants give way in ranks of succession: at the highest part of the intertidal zone, Pacific cinquefoil and water parsnip are dominant; farther out, where water swamps the vegetation for many hours a day, sedge becomes more common, until it stretches before the eyes like a prairie pasture.

Over the waving sedge fields swallows dip and dive, erratically chasing flying insects. Soon they'll begin gathering nervously on the telephone wires, filling the air with their electric chatter as they group for the southerly migration. Swallows are among the first of the resident birds to leave and are a reminder that fall is not far off.

High above me I see a flock of small gulls soaring on the hot midday thermals, rising like hawks. They are mew gulls, feeding on flying insects while they wait for the year's great feast of salmon carcasses to begin.

Opening in the sea of grass now and again are channel pools that I have to splash through, sending schools of small fish diving for cover. Sculpins dart into the mud, leaving only a puff of sediment behind them. These bottom-dwelling fish are easily recognized by their large heads and large fanlike pectoral fins. A study in nearby Hook Nose Creek revealed there were enough sculpins in the stream to consume 500,000 pink and chum salmon fry each year.

Juvenile salmon and trout are often trapped in these estuary channel pools at low tide and must be quick to avoid the attacks of sculpins and birds. Despite its many dangers, the estuary provides an important rearing habitat for young salmon. All salmon and trout of the Bella Coola River spend at least some time in the brackish waters of the estuary before heading out to the open ocean.

The estuary is where fresh water mixes with salt water, and it is where the river finally slows, dropping suspended particles of mud, silt, sand and larger debris, such as dead salmon. In the shallow, relatively warm waters, microscopic floating plants known as phytoplankton thrive on the abundant nutrients. Estuaries are among the richest ecosystems in the world—rivalling tropical rain forests, coastal temperate rain forests and coral reefs for productivity. The average coastal estuary grows 7 or more tonnes of vegetation per hectare per year—more than a fertilized cornfield. It is this capacity to produce so much organic material that makes coastal estuaries so important to so many different species. Everything from grizzly bears to deer grazes on the vegetation that grows in the intertidal zone.

When the various salmon smolts arrive at the mouth of the Bella Coola they find an abundance of plankton, invertebrates and small fish to feed on. Here the young salmon congregate in schools and grow rapidly for a few weeks. The different salmon and trout species seem to use the estuary at slightly different times, corresponding roughly to their smolting schedule.

After half an hour of picking my way carefully northwest through the tide flats, I finally find the banks of the Bella Coola River. The current is moving fast but will slow as the tide rises against it. You can sense the energy the river unleashes.

The Bella Coola flows out of sight through a broad, expansive mud flat, which is dotted with stumps and logs and the occasional hummock of sediment. Beyond the flats, which you can't cross because of the depth of the silt, lie the dark waters of the ocean.

In the distance a flock of sandpipers runs across the soft mud, stopping to quickly feed, then scurrying on. In the shallows of the river a female merganser trails a brood of nineteen, probably the offspring of two or more hens. It's bird daycare; the other female will be somewhere nearby. The flock splashes loudly as the birds run across the surface. The young haven't learned to fly yet, and the adults are in moult.

The Bella Coola is seasonally high and thickly coloured with glacial flour. Visibility is so low that my fly disappears after sinking only a few centimetres in the chalky water. The silt consists mainly of tiny granitic particles formed by the abrasion of glaciers over the peaks of the Coast Mountains, far up the Talchako River. If it were not for the silt, the Bella Coola River would be an even more productive salmon and trout stream. The silt colours the Bella Coola for up to six months of every year, reducing the amount of light that reaches the river bottom and limiting plant and algae growth. Decreased plant production means decreased aquatic insect production, which in turn means decreased production of fish.

The surface of the sea stirs, and as I watch, waves of pink salmon come into sight and then boldly plunge into the coloured waters of the Bella Coola River. I can see their grey backs jostling together at times as they shoulder their way into the river. Instinctively they know that upstream, through the gritty water, they will find clear tributaries to spawn in. Most of the pinks will run quickly upstream to join the sockeye, chinook and a few early coho and summer steelhead already holding in the Atnarko River.

Close to shore, a pair of dog salmon appears, big and rough beside the sleek, compact pinks. Most of the chums are headed for the mouths of tributaries in the lower 30 kilometres of the valley. For both pink and chum, spawning begins around mid-August, peaking in September.

I have come to catch pinks and am lightly equipped with a five-weight fly rod that is perfect for small fish. I don't want to hook a chum on this outfit. Chum are the junkyard dogs of the salmon world, with their thick shoulders, calico colouring and protruding canine teeth. They are probably the most aggressive salmon you can find in fresh water. While a pink will take a fly in the firm, soft manner of a trout, chum always seem to hook up running. And they aren't stopped easily. If it weren't for the fact that chum are discoloured almost from the moment they enter a river, they would have long ago been recognized as one of British Columbia's greatest game fish.

Chum begin their spawning transformation as soon as they enter Burke Channel, where they get the first taste of the Bella Coola River. Despite the fact that chum salmon migrate up the channel at up to 50 kilometres a day, by the time they hit the river obvious morphological changes have already taken place. Their metallic blue backs have turned black, and their bright silver sides are green with reddish-purple stains shaped like flames. The males develop a hooked nose and large doglike teeth (hence the name dog salmon). To some, they are not attractive fish at all, but there is a primitive, fascinating beauty to them. And there is no disputing their brute strength. They fight even as you try to unhook them, banging their big tails against your legs and wrenching themselves out of your hands with powerful twists of their bodies. Chum average about 5.5 kilograms, but the world record was caught in the Bella Coola estuary, in 1951—it weighed 15 kilograms and was 100 centimetres long. If you hooked a fish like that on a fly the only question would be whether your rod shattered or your reel melted.

The river often has a run of 1 million pinks and has had returns pushing 3 million. But stocks have fallen as low as 250,000, and because of the enormous commercial harvest, which takes over 50 per cent of the run, there is always a danger the population could be knocked down. Fisheries managers often miscalculate run sizes, sometimes by a million or more fish, and don't have much of a margin for error, despite the apparent health of the pink population.

Sitting on an old log that has been bleached by the sun and cast up by the tide, I watch pinks rolling on the surface. It is a mesmerizing show of abundance. Every few seconds a fish jumps out of the water, landing with a fluttering splash. When pink and chum salmon return to the estuary, they characteristically spend a few days getting used to fresh water before heading upstream. Gathering in the brackish broth of the river mouth allows their bodies time to adjust to the radical osmotic differences that exist between salt and fresh water.

On large streams such as the Bella Coola River, the lower pools will contain fish that have just arrived with the tide, as well as those that have been holding for a few days. As new fish arrive, those that have adapted to the change will move upstream. Sometimes huge, dense schools collect in pools. It is easy to tell when pink salmon are around because they are constantly jumping, typically landing on their sides, in a fluttering, distinctive splash. Chum land the same way but fall back with a heavy crash. No one seems to know why fish jump; some biologists think they are trying to rid themselves of sea lice, others argue that the fish are orienting themselves to their surroundings, and others say that jumping helps salmon acclimatize to the freshwater environment. Whatever the cause, it helps you locate them, particularly in silty water. But jumpers don't always bite.

Pinks have become increasingly popular as a sports fish and for good reason. Caught fresh from the sea, they are strong fighters and they are good to eat. They are also often available in such numbers that a fly-fisher can catch dozens of them a day. Sometimes they sulk and won't take a fly for hours. But then they suddenly turn on and you get strike after strike.

Hot-pink flies are all the rage for pinks, but they will take many patterns, from small green nymphs, fished at a dead drift, to minnow imitations. My favourite is a teal-and-silver fly with a red throat. Not only do pinks take it, but so do sea-run cutthroat and steelhead.

Wading hip deep in the river, I start by quartering the fly across the current on a sink tip. Several casts are retrieved in steady foot-long pulls. When that fails, I try a slower, more erratic series of short pulls and pauses to imitate the jerky movement of a shrimp. Though pinks, like all salmon, stop eating once they enter fresh water, a feeding reflex can be triggered, especially when they are just in from the sea. The longer the fish is in fresh water, the harder it is to trigger the reflex.

As my eyes wander to the dramatic black cliff on the far side of the river, I feel a slow, delicate, pluck on the end of my line. When the hook is set a salmon responds with two quick leaps, a short run downstream and another upstream. In a few minutes a pink comes in, bright silver on the sides with a clean white belly. Sea lice are clinging to its side, just ahead of the tail. A quick release—and a few casts later another salmon takes the fly. It holds deep, and I feel the current thrumming against the line. Then it makes a run, turns, zips back across in the other direction and comes up in a series of splashy jumps. It's a twin of the first, about 2 kilograms. Before a half-hour is over, six more salmon have come to the riverbank and been released. Sometimes when the fish run I can feel the line hitting other salmon in the school.

Moving upstream I see the tails and backs of chum close to the shore, and for some reason I cast to them. Call it the hunting reflex. I know instantly that I've made a mistake because one of the chum salmon turns on the fly with a sudden, violent swing of its head—and is away in the current. He runs out, gathers the full force of the Bella Coola River against his broad side and rips line off my reel at a frightening speed in a diagonal run downstream. Making a turn that leaves a huge boil on the surface, the salmon goes up past me again, picks up the slack before I have a chance to reel in and runs 30 metres straight on. The rod is vibrating and jumping up and down and the reel handle is spinning so fast I don't dare touch it. I just let him go. The last of the fly line is off the reel and the backing is quickly unwinding. Then the fish stops, and wading and stumbling, I regain some line. Half a dozen runs later, the fish finally quits. I push the rod to its limit to lift his head out, and the current turns him back towards me. The chum lies in the shallows, disoriented for a moment, and I quickly lean over and twist the hook loose, being careful to avoid his sharp teeth. He is gone in a blast of water, vanishing into the silty current like a shooting star.

To the old Nuxalk, August was known not for the mystery in the heavens but for the movement in the river that brought them their favourite salmon. August is Si7ist'lilhh, or Dog Salmon Moon. In the old days chum were the preferred catch of the Nuxalk because their low fat content makes them the best fish of all the salmon to smoke. Cutting the fish into strips, or simply splitting it in half, they would dry it on racks in the sun, a smouldering, smoking fire staining the flesh and preparing it for the cold winter months ahead. A properly smoked salmon would last all year. You can take a slab of chum, smoked as stiff as leather, and rest it skin-side down on a grill over a campfire. As it warms it unfurls, what oils are left are released, and within minutes you have a salmon feast.

But dark times have fallen on the river, for some Nuxalk have become contemptuous of chum and of pink salmon, which were also once highly valued. You can walk through the small town of Bella Coola, down past the old church and a weatherworn motel, to where the Native housing stands, facing the river. Once there were longhouses lined up here, with elaborate thunderbird and grizzly bear motifs painted on them, but today there are modern single-family homes, with pickup trucks and satellite dishes.

The houses still look out over the river, where Native drift boats come down, as they always have. Usually there are two men, one on the oars, the other hauling the net and picking out the salmon. You can hear the big fish thump on the floorboards. Often the men will pull ashore here to sort their salmon. The valuable coho are carefully put aside—but the chum and the pink salmon are thrown away, tossed end over end into the shallows.

Gulls gather nervously, lifting their wings in excitement as they waddle along the gravel bars to attack the dead or dying fish. Eagles hunch on the branches of nearby trees waiting for the boatmen to leave. Every fifteen or twenty minutes another drift boat appears, and frequently the ritual of waste is repeated. The fishers often keep only the coho, which draw a higher price on the market.

Watching this sad procession, I calculate that Native fishers are capable of killing—and throwing away—hundreds of pink and chum salmon a day. Walking the river bank, I soon count fifty dead salmon that are too fresh from the sea to have spawned. I retrieve two big chum, chasing away a flock of gulls before they have a chance to rip into them. When I cut them open great handfuls of golden eggs spill out. Later I brine and smoke the fish. They are good eating, the flesh rich and sweet. Once the Nuxalk knew that taste—and they ate the meat of the great dogs with appreciation. Today many see salmon only as "pieces," chunks of flesh that can be sold for cash.

Federal fisheries officers patrol the Bella Coola River, as they do on other important salmon streams in British Columbia, but they have a lot of water to cover. And there is not a lot of pressure for increased enforcement. In the New Age, Native people have attained an untouchable status in the eyes of some. Perhaps it would be difficult to enforce the law on the river and arrest and charge all those guilty of such waste. But I know there are many Nuxalk who would quietly welcome such action. Traditional Nuxalk elders believe it is an insult to the Creator to catch something and waste it. According to legend, the Creator will stop providing for the people if they waste the fish they take from the river.

It can be argued that if the Nuxalk were allowed to build a weir on the river, of the kind they once had, none of this waste need happen. Only the salmon that were wanted could be killed; the rest could pass upstream.

These great fish, which have come home from a distant ocean, following the stars, have passed for centuries virtually under the doorsteps of the Nuxalk. To kill them and throw them aside like rags is a crime against nature.

At night you can stand on the banks of the Bella Coola River listening to the rustle of the current, knowing the sound is timeless. Sometimes you might see the reflection of a shooting star and hear a salmon, ripping the current. You might say that's a dog, or that's a pink. But all you know for sure is that the river is running and the salmon are running in it, completing a transect between the heavens and the sea.

September

Coho Salmon Moon

The ghost of the forest hangs over the valley. All that is left of what was once an old-growth forest, a great cascade of greenness that poured down from the mountains to the sea, is the smoke from slash, burned by forest managers. The huge, sweeping branches of the fragrant cedar, the scaly bark of the spruce, the shattered trunks of giant, rotting Douglas fir and the gentle, whiplike arms of the western hemlock are all being reduced to cinder and ash. The fires will help enrich the soil and soon a replanted forest will spring to life, but it will take a thousand years to grow back a forest the equal of the one that has been removed, and some say it will never be the same. The plan is to log again in another sixty to one hundred years. By then a new generation of British Columbians may be more questioning of logging practices—but they will never know what the forest was really like or understand how it was lost.

Towards the end of the month, on September 22, sunlight

and darkness will be divided equally. And then the days will shorten, the nights will grow longer, and winter will not be far behind. The birds are the first to sense this change, and their migrations begin, triggered by declining daylight, diminished food supplies and the sudden coldness of the nights. One day as you go down to the river you can look up to see clouds of violet-green swallows soaring over the water. The next day, the sky is empty. Of the ninety bird species that spend the summer in the Bella Coola Valley, over fifty will have left by month's end. Flying at 30 kilometres per hour, some may go up to 1900 kilometres before they are forced to stop and feed again. By then the Bella Coola Valley will be just a memory, a resonant spark of instinct in their brains that will guide them back in the spring. The yellow warbler, brown-headed cowbird, rufous hummingbird, western flycatcher, Vaux's swift, black-headed grosbeak, western tanager, Swainson's thrush and common nighthawk are all among the first to depart, some leaving in the final days of August. Soon they will nearly all be gone, as will some of the bats, moths and butterflies that also migrate. Many of the small bird species leave at night, and so you never see the flocks departing. Gradually you become aware of their absence. The larger birds, the ducks and geese, are impossible to miss as they head south in ragged Vs, their calls echoing with undefined yearning. In eight months the birds will return from wintering grounds as far away as Argentina. But as they go, you can't help but feel a sense of loss.

Still, the river drives on, undiminished. The pools are feverish with the spawning activities of chum, pink and chinook salmon. In some places the banks are littered with post-spawn carcasses, and the river has taken on a rich, lingering smell. In the shallows, salmon that were burnished just a few weeks ago are showing the ragged cloak of death. Tails and fins are worn; skin grows mossy with infection of saprolegnia or furunculosis.

Shouldering into this rich and chaotic scene is what many regard as the most exciting run of them all—the coho, a sleek, solid salmon with bright silver sides and eyes that have a wild look to them.

Coho feed aggressively at sea, almost as if they were rushing to build up their energy stores in anticipation of their spectacular spawning run. When they first arrive back in fresh water, it seems as if they are hot-wired to attack any prey. They will take big bright streamers, in clear water sometimes swerving well off their course to seize the fly. And they will take tiny wet flies, fished through a run at dead drift, as you would when casting for resident rainbows. When hooked, they run at tremendous speed, jumping, tail-walking and sometimes going end over end in crazy tumbles. I once lost a fresh coho when it broke the line by jumping over a tree branch that was hanging more than a metre above the surface.

Although adult coho actually begin returning to the Bella Coola River in mid-August, September (Si7iswaylhh) is when the migration peaks. The earliest coho appear to be headed to the headwaters of the Atnarko River, while those that arrive later spawn mostly in the lower end of the system.

After a week or two in the river, coho begin to transform from metallic blue and silver into spawning colours. The males become darker and develop red sides with bluish-green backs and heads. The upper jaw becomes strongly hooked and teeth become enlarged, although they don't have the rabid dog appearance of chum. The spawning females are not as vivid as the males, and the jaw is much less hooked. Spawning starts by October, peaking in November, and some fish are still active as late as February.

Coho spawning resembles that of other salmon. The female selects a nest site, testing the current with her body and sometimes stirring the gravel, as if to inspect its quality. Typically, she and her mates will defend an area of about 12 metres square. Above and below her, other females establish nesting territories, while males fight and jockey for position to determine who is dominant. The female digs a nest by rolling onto her side and vigorously flexing her body and tail. Although it appears that she is beating the gravel, she is using the upward flex to create a current that lifts rocks from the bottom. A depression is created —a nest of stones. When she is ready a male, usually the largest and most aggressive one in the area, lies beside her. He shimmies against her, nudges her and then releases a cloud of milt as her slightly adhesive eggs simultaneously fall into the depression.

Afterwards the female moves upstream to dig another nest. Much of the gravel she stirs will fall back to cover the first nest. She will spawn several times, sometimes with just one male, sometimes with different partners. The series of nests she builds are collectively known as a redd. She will deposit about 800 eggs in each nest, laying down about 2500 in all. Over 75 per cent of her eggs will fall safely into a nest; the rest will be swept away by the current. It's not uncommon during the spawn to see eggs scattered among the stones, where trout and char, which have trailed the salmon upstream, feed on them.

The spawned-out female defends her redd until she is too weak to hold a position in the current. Then she drifts gently downstream, her skin tarnished by spreading bacterial infection, and dies. A female lasts five to fifteen days after spawning; a male lives five to thirty days.

Now the brutal attrition begins. The percentage of fertilized eggs that survive varies from year to year, depending on winter floods, the grinding effect of bottom ice, predation by birds, insects and fish, and the smothering effect of silt. Typically, from 15 to 30 per cent of eggs survive, hatching in early spring. The fry emerge from the gravel about three weeks later. After a winter or two in the river, the coho smolts migrate to the ocean, where they begin a period of rapid growth.

Despite heavy predation, the survival rate for coho after they hit the estuary is high compared with that of other salmon species. Typically, 5 per cent to 15 per cent survive—three to ten times the rate of other salmon species.

Studies in the Bella Coola estuary have shown that coho smolts feed heavily on pink fry during the first few weeks. After about forty days, however, most pink fry have grown large enough to avoid coho. It is believed that this relationship, over time, has reinforced the characteristics that make Bella Coola pink salmon such a fast-growing species. The fish that grow slowly have been systematically removed from the genetic mix.

After a few months in the estuary, schools of young coho move out to coastal waters, expanding their diet to include herring, anchovies, surf smelts, sand lance, sticklebacks, sardines, capelins, rockfish, sablefish, lantern fish, Pacific sauries, hake and pollock.

Depending on the local abundance of food and perhaps on their specific genetic makeup, Bella Coola coho will either spend their entire adult lives feeding in local outside waters (for example, Fitz Hugh Sound or Queen Charlotte Sound) or undertake longer northerly migrations, into the Gulf of Alaska. Tagging studies reveal that migratory coho will travel up to 1600 kilometres northwesterly before heading in a counterclockwise direction back to their home spawning streams, twelve to eighteen months later. Travelling and feeding in the upper 27 metres of the ocean, homeward-bound coho cover 30 to 55 kilometres a day.

Most returning Bella Coola coho weigh 2.7 to 5.4 kilograms, but many anglers hook fish that exceed 7 kilograms, the size at which they become known as northern coho, or simply northerns. Studies suggest that the larger fish became smolts earlier and returned as adults later than the average coho. They are bigger simply because they have spent longer feeding in the rich ocean.

At sea coho are a prime target for both commercial and sports fleets—and they are intercepted all along the coast, particularly early in the summer, when they are feeding heavily in bays and inlets. A favourite place to find coho is near kelp beds, where they are pursuing herring. Sometimes herring will be corralled by a school of coho in a bay or in the scalloped face of a cliff, and the salmon will hold there for days. When word gets out, the sports fleet converges on them. In many areas, coho have been fished too heavily by commercial fleets and their natal streams have been degraded by development, leading to the total collapse of runs.

Coho have become the number one game fish in the Bella Coola River because they are more abundant and fight almost as well as steelhead. Bella Coola coho are now the preferred target for most local guides, as hundred of sports anglers make annual trips to the valley in the fall in hopes of catching one of the famous northerns.

Peak sports fishing for coho is between the last week of September and the third week in October. The river is clearing, the water level is falling, and the fish are entering the river in high numbers. And because they move quickly through the system, fresh bright coho can be encountered just about anywhere.

Silver coho covered with sea lice have been caught in the lower Atnarko, meaning that some fish are making the 60-kilometre trip from the estuary in less than two days.

Going down to the river on a smoky, bright day, I see that the foliage has turned from a lush green to a mix of reds, yellows and browns. The maple is as scarlet as a sockeye, the alder has taken on a soft golden glow, and the thimbleberry leaves are turning burnt orange. When the wind blows now there is a gentle rattling sound.

Rays of sunlight cut through the smoky haze that hangs in the valley. Fireweed fluff, floating spider webs and millions of flying insects glint in the light, shimmering against the backdrop of a dark coniferous forest.

In a nearby mountain ash, robins and starlings are feeding heavily on bright orange berries. On the valley floor the peak of the berry crop is past, but higher up the hillsides saskatoons, bunchberries, huckleberries, gooseberries, baneberries and purple queen's cup are just starting to ripen. The late blooming of the fruit towards the top of the mountains coincides with the migration of many bird species.

In the valley, berries have ripened in waves over the summer. If all the berries peaked at once in the valley, animals would be overwhelmed by the abundance and many berries would rot. And once the berry crop was finished there would be nothing to sustain the fruit eaters through the long summer. The consequences would be disastrous for both plants and animals.

High on the hillsides, however, a different strategy of mass ripening makes sense. During this time, hundreds of thousands of birds are passing along the mountaintops. They stop to gorge on the berry crop and then move on. It is almost as if the plants know that their seeds will be consumed in a frenzy of feeding in the fall. As the birds move, they carry the seeds of the fruit with them to the next alpine stop.

As I wade down to fish below Thorsen Creek, pink salmon, dazed and exhausted by the spawning ritual, bump against my legs. They are no longer the bright silver fish they were when they first arrived from the sea. Now they are the colour of old stones. Farther downstream I notice a clump of fish drifting unnaturally near the shore. They are tangled in the deadly black lace of a drift net. The mesh has caught them behind the gills, killing them as they struggled to escape. They are twisted and stiff. There are forty pinks and ten chum in the net; some of them have been there so long they are beginning to decompose. I rip the net from its mooring on the shore and slash gaping holes in the webbing. It makes no sense to do so, but I cut the dead fish loose and put them back in the river. Then I drag the net up on the bank, tangle it with driftwood and kick it into the bushes.

It is a Nuxalk "food fishery" net and what I have done may be illegal, but if the law protects this sort of practice, it deserves to be broken. Eggs and milt spilled from the dead salmon. All that way, that great journey out to sea, all those dangers overcome—for such a tragic, wasteful ending. Whoever owned the net had set it in a spawning area, apparently hoping to catch a few fresh coho and not caring about the peripheral damage. Wading out into the Bella Coola, I stoop to wash the fish slime and blood from my hands. They are tender from where I'd gripped the net. Later I would still hear the ringing sound my knife blade made every time it cut a strand of nylon. If the world has any sense, I think, nets like that would simply be banned.

The river is still clouded with silt and I wade gingerly, feeling for the edge of a bar to fish into the deeper holding water below. Every few minutes I see the back of a coho break the surface, slick and glistening and muscled. Some of the coho are so bright it's clear they have just come in on the morning tide, and they seem bound on steaming upstream. Others may have been here a few days and are holding. The fish that stay will later move up into Thorsen Creek, where they will spawn after fall rains have swollen the creek and its small tributaries.

The waters of Thorsen are clear, but soon they are swallowed by the grey waters of the main river. Every now and then I see a fish roll along a seam where the two waters meet. Visibility in the Bella Coola is only about 30 centimetres, but the bulk of the fish seem to be holding on the dark side of the seam, in the main current. I tie on a streamer that looks like a small herring, using a sink tip line and a leader only half a metre long. The cast is quartered upstream to give the fly time to sink before it swings back towards the clear waters of Thorsen. On the fourth cast there is a solid knock, and a lively fish turns to run with the fly. At first I think it's a coho jack, a sexually mature salmon that has come in early from the sea. Jacks, which return after only four to six months in the ocean, do participate in spawning, but it isn't known what their role is. Some believe they are a safety check, there to provide sperm in the absence of any big males; others think they are a nuisance that introduces inferior genes. They are spirited fish that are often bright silver and usually weigh a kilogram or so.

As I draw the fish in I see that it isn't a jack but a big, 53-centimetre cutthroat. The fish is heavy through the belly and may weigh 2 kilograms. There is little sign of the characteristic cutthroat mark under the jaw—just a pale pink slash. On the sides are two small sea lice, showing that the fish has come from the estuary within the last forty-eight hours.

For an hour I work the water without another hit. There are

coho around, but I am either missing them or they simply aren't in the mood to take. Then, on a cast that is no different from the others, there is a solid pull as the fly comes around below me. I miss the strike and quickly cast again. This time I bring the fly back in short, rapid jerks, trying to imitate a fleeing bait fish. It works. Six metres below me a V forms on the surface behind the fly. It is the unmistakable waking chase of large salmon. I stop the retrieve—and the fish takes the fly with a huge swirl, his dorsal fin and back showing clearly as he strikes.

In the big, brawling current of the Bella Coola, a strong, fast salmon is always a challenge. A coho is a revelation. The fish runs diagonally upstream for 30 metres, then jumps, shaking its head as it falls back into the water. The fish runs again, going deep into the backing and moving so fast that the line hisses through the water. It jumps and crashes at the end of the run and then turns and comes sweeping back with the current. Its next run is shorter, and then it holds in the current, in a test of strength against the bowed fly rod. Finally it wallows on the surface and then holds close to the bank while I wade up to it. It is a big male, hook jawed, its belly white. Its back has a prismatic purple sheen that looks like sunlight refracted from the bottom of the ocean. I hold it by the tail, unhook it and wait until it pushes itself away. It vanishes, trailing whorls of silt behind it.

Before I can cast again a Nuxalk drift boat comes down through the fast run above me and pulls into shore. It trails a gill net, and as the boat bumps against the rocks, one of the boatmen jumps out and hauls the net ashore. They pick the salmon quickly, throwing about half a dozen coho into the boat.

The Nuxalk used to get all the coho they needed by drifting the lower 6 kilometres of the Bella Coola River. But as stocks declined and the selling of "food fish" became legal under federal law, Native fishers began to take their nets farther and farther upstream so that they could sweep more of the river. They were entrepreneurs now, out to convert salmon into cash.

At one time the smaller tributaries of the lower Bella Coola were among the most important spawning sites in the whole system. The coho would hold in the main river until the water level rose; then they would begin to make their way back into the forest, following a lacework of streams. By November and December the coho had gone over the beaver dams and up the smallest tributaries. By moving farther upstream with their drift nets, the Nuxalk began killing more of the coho before they could escape up the side streams. Habitat destruction in the lower valley, by farmers and developers who filled in wetlands or built dikes, compounded the problem. And all the while sports and commercial fishers fished the coho intensively. In the beaver dam pools coho fry soon became noticeably absent.

In one of those bureaucratic decisions that defy understanding, the federal government's department of fisheries chose this crucial juncture to cancel a coho enhancement program run by the Snootli Hatchery. Under the program—which cost only $10,000 a year—about 45,000 adult coho were being produced annually.

On many rivers, hatchery programs have been counterproductive because hatchery-reared salmon grow faster under controlled conditions and are better at competing for feeding space. Thus, the hatchery fish bully the wild stock out of the best feeding sites. But hatchery salmon have a much harder time surviving in the ocean, so increased numbers of the hatchery fish often lead, over time, to a decline in stocks. The Snootli program, however, held its coho until they were smolts, releasing them as the wild stock exited the river. That way the hatchery and wild stock weren't thrown into competition in the river.

At one time government biologists believed that the Bella Coola system could support a spawning run of 80,000 coho. A target of 50,000 was established as a reasonable goal. In 1982, a state of emergency was declared because the number of coho reaching the spawning grounds was averaging less than 15,000 fish. The Snootli Hatchery was asked to begin enhancement of Bella Coola coho, and soon stocks were on the rebound. The original plan was to use the hatchery to build stocks back up to historical levels. But by the early 1990s, there were still only 15,000 to 21,000 coho returning to the spawning beds.

Despite the success of the Snootli Hatchery program, the coho run was kept low by overfishing. While the enhancement program was producing bigger runs, it was also fuelling an increased demand for fish by Native, commercial and sports fishers. The catch rates climbed. The Department of Fisheries and Oceans had developed a hatchery program that worked—but then had failed to link it to a long-term management plan that brought the user groups under control. And in the end, government did the inexplicable—it cancelled the enhancement program.

Coho stocks are now in desperate straits in the Bella Coola and could soon become as endangered as the steelhead. Although genetically the coho might be better off without a hatchery, the cold reality is that the appetite for coho among the sports, commercial and Native fisheries will not diminish, even though the program has ended. The result can be only a sharp decline in the number of returning spawners. Unless there is a corresponding drop in fishing, both wild and enhanced stocks will be devastated.

In an average year commercial fishers kill 32,000 Bella Coola coho as they make their way south from Alaska and into Burke Channel. The Nuxalk take fewer than two thousand, while sports anglers kill about five hundred. After all groups have taken their share, fewer than nineteen thousand coho are left to spawn. Without augmentation, that number will drop rapidly.

It took only a few moments for the Nuxalk gill-netters to pick their net and rebundle it for the next leg of the drift. Soon they had gone out of sight below me. I stood and watched the river but couldn't bring myself to cast again. Going back up Thorsen towards the road, I saw a place where a bear had dragged some salmon high onto the bank. It had eaten only their brains, a common practice in times of abundance. Later in the year the bears would be happy with old carcasses.

Salmon carcasses have washed up on gravel bars, or they've drifted to the bottom of the deeper pools and caught on snags. Most the fish on shore have been broken open by birds, accelerating decomposition. Each scavenger seems to have its own preference at this time of year. Some recently killed salmon are missing only their eyes—obviously pecked out by crows, ravens and gulls. The outer skin of salmon fed on by otters is peeled away from the muscle mass. There are scattered bones and bits of flesh everywhere. Upstream several bald eagles tear apart salmon carcasses, fussing like vultures. It is said that the eagle, this "noblest of birds," prefers its salmon four to six weeks dead.

There are bear tracks on every sandbar. A week earlier an angler had been run off Thorsen Creek by an angry sow with cubs. Bears now are to be expected anywhere along the river. Up and down the valley both black and grizzly bears are congregating to feed on salmon. Studies have shown that some bears will catch as many as eight salmon an hour as they binge. For them, surviving the winter will depend on whether or not they can build up enough fat reserves to get through hibernation. Pregnant female bears require abundant stores of fat. Pregnancy, birth and nursing will consume up to a kilogram of fat a day. By the time spring rolls around, a bear will have lost as much as 40 per cent of its autumn body weight.

In the days when salmon runs were naturally plentiful, rotting carcasses clogged every conceivable spawning stream up and down the coast. The amount of nitrogen, carbon, phosphorus and other nutrients contained in the dead fish was enormous. The salmon migration is nature's way of transferring nutrients from the rich ocean environment to the relatively impoverished ecosystem in the river. The fish not only directly feed other animals, such as bears and eagles, but also perform an invaluable role by fertilizing the watershed. The impact of industrial fishing is not understood—but it is clear that by reducing the salmon runs by half, we have reduced the amount of fertilizer by half. Any gardener would argue that eventually there will have to be a cost in reduced productivity. And surely that decline will be reflected not just in the size of subsequent salmon runs but also in the populations of other animals that depend on salmon.

Farmers routinely rotate crops, allowing their fields a chance to recover from intense use. But when was the last time anyone ever said: "Let's close this river to fishing for a few cycles to let the salmon revitalize the ecosystem"?

On the trail out I pass Bob "the Butcher" and his wife, carrying large spinning rods. Bob comes to the Bella Coola Valley to fish for coho and sea-run cutthroat every fall. Local fly-fishers gave him his nickname because he kills everything he catches. He's an effective angler. Many people think Bob is a charitable guy because he gives away a lot of fish. Me, I think he is a sociopath who kills salmon as indiscriminately as a gill net. His generosity is a form of ego.

"Any luck?" he asks in a jovial voice.

"Not a damn thing," I say.

"Well, nice day anyway," he says with a laugh. "Think we'll give it a try."

"Yeah, well, look out for the bear ..." I say, hoping the warning will nag him into leaving early.

As I sit on the truck tailgate, feeling weighed down by my waders, I am struck by the silence of the forest. The smell of smoke fills the air. I hold the fly in my palm. It is still wet from the water inside a coho's mouth, which seems a miraculous thing.

October

Moon When Fern Root Is Gathered

As the days grow colder and snow creeps down towards the tree line, the glaciers stop melting. Far below, silt settles out of the Bella Coola River and the water takes on a deep blue-green tint. The river becomes the colour of the forest—of Sitka spruce drenched in rain. All along the Pacific coast in October a series of storms are unleashed, bringing heavy downpours and high winds. Autumn rains coax salamanders and frogs from their moist summer hiding places and trigger an explosion of mushrooms, starting a feverish harvest by local residents.

In the valley the small streams swell, the beaver ponds overflow, and the coho, smaller and darker than they were a few weeks earlier, begin to move onto their spawning beds. The fishing season is tailing off, but there are still places where resident river trout, grown fat from gorging on salmon eggs, will rise to a surface fly. And a steelhead, a glinting, gemlike salmon from the remnants of a once great summer run, might yet be found, somewhere in the unknowable mystery of the river.

Driving up the Bella Coola Valley towards the Atnarko River, in search of resident trout that local anglers call the slab-sided rainbow, I am struck by the rich, pungent smell in the air. The salmon carcasses are being subsumed by the environment, and a more subtle, earthy scent is emerging. Heavy winds and rains have stripped most deciduous trees of their leaves, and now the forest floor is strewn with a dark brown carpet of decomposing vegetation. For many people, the odour of decay is the smell of the hunt. Throughout the valley, rifles are being taken down from wall racks, their firing mechanisms oiled, their sights zeroed in. Soon, in a ritual that seems as old as the valley itself, hunters will begin searching the snowy subalpine meadows for mule deer, the bucks heavy with rut. Or, climbing higher, they will seek out the mountain goats, which shine like flecks of mica against the black granite cliffs. Only the toughest and most energetic local hunters will try to go high above the tree line to stalk the white-robed goats, which avoid most predation simply by living in high, dangerous places.

Although hunting is dismissed by many as a blood sport, it must be noted that hunters pay their own way—unlike the present commercial salmon fishery, which is heavily subsidized by the Canadian taxpayer. It is estimated that hunters inject more than $245 million annually into the economy in their pursuit of wildlife in British Columbia. In addition, they pay more than $10 million a year for licences. Over and above that, they contribute voluntarily. The British Columbia Wildlife Federation spent more than $5.5 million to enhance habitat in 1995, while Ducks Unlimited has spent over $55 million in British Columbia in recent years. Despite the obvious economic benefits associated with hunting, surveys show that the majority of North Americans don't support killing wildlife for sport. Many people believe that the killing of animals by hunters is cruel and unnecessary.

In contrast, the general public does support the notion of mass killing of domestic animals for food (in slaughterhouses), and it does support the concept of commercial fisheries, which kill tens of millions of wild salmon every year on the Pacific coast. Some people disdain hunting, but humans eat a lot of meat.

Commercial hunting was ended because it was wasteful and destructive. Increasingly, parallels are being drawn to commercial salmon fishing. In the 1800s professional hunters shot, netted, harpooned and bludgeoned billions of animals to death in the name of profit. The relentless efficiency of these professional hunters was amazing. In less than one hundred years, humans somehow managed to kill two billion passenger pigeons, one million Eskimo curlews and thousands of eastern elk, Merriam's elk and Audubon's bighorn sheep, all of which were hunted to extinction. Professional hunters also managed to kill tens of millions of buffalo and other big game animals, as well as hundreds of thousands of sea otters, beavers and whales.

In addition to the killing of animals for food and fur, millions of birds were shot indiscriminately as part of a thriving plume trade, which, for one bizarre period, featured not just feathers stuck to hats but entire birds. Cedar waxwings, northern flickers, snow buntings, northern bobwhites, common terns, snowy egrets and trumpeter swans were hunted ruthlessly—for fashion.

Because of this widespread slaughter, resource managers at the end of the 1800s were faced with a dilemma. Should they continue as they had and risk the extermination of many species, or should they change the philosophy behind hunting? After a great deal of debate, they chose to force change upon an unwilling sector of society. Biologists decided it would be better to sell the right to hunt wildlife for sport rather than to continue slaughtering it for sale.

In both Canada and the United States, governments made it illegal to market meat or parts of game animals, shorebirds and songbirds. By outlawing the lucrative market for wildlife, government biologists in effect took the value out of dead things. Only living wildlife had value—and that value could be realized through selling the right to hunt. Next, they clearly outlined, by law, how wildlife would be killed. They purposely made killing wildlife economically unrewarding; as any hunter knows, it is cheaper to buy meat at the store than it is to get it in the field. Finally, government biologists made it illegal to kill wildlife frivolously. Sustenance hunting was recognized as a priority, and hunting was prohibited wherever wildlife populations were in decline. To ensure that there would always be habitat for big game animals, Canada and the United States set aside national parks, wildlife refuges and ecological reserves. Hunting was also restricted throughout most of the year to allow wildlife to breed and raise their young, sustaining populations in the face of growing threats to their existence.

It wasn't an easy sell. The plume industry claimed that 83,000 workers would be plunged into destitution. Many hunters objected because they would no longer be allowed to kill animals wherever and whenever they wanted. Thankfully, the government biologists ignored the protests and chose to conserve North American wildlife. The implementation of regulations prevented the extinction of some bison subspecies, musk oxen, wood ducks, trumpeter swans, snowy egrets, whooping cranes and numerous songbird species.

Since commercial hunting was banned, the numbers of most big game animals have increased. There are over 30 million big game animals in North America today, and deer populations are at an all-time high. There are even viable populations of large predators (wolves, bears, wolverines and cougars in some areas) —something many countries cannot even imagine. Where game populations are threatened, industrial activity, not hunting, is largely to blame.

Despite such dramatic evidence against the commercial harvest of wild creatures, there are still thousands of people making a living today as salmon fishers off the Pacific coast of North America. They have netted billions of salmon and trout, contributing to the extermination of hundreds of wild stocks in California, Oregon, Idaho, Washington, British Columbia and Alaska. Hundreds more stocks are listed as being at high risk of extinction—and even in areas of abundance, such as the Fraser River, salmon stocks are at half their historical levels.

In British Columbia there are about 530 purse seiners, 1500 gill-net boats, 1500 trollers and 750 fishing vessels that can both gill-net and troll. It is worth pointing out that 140 purse seiners are owned by companies that also operate huge retail food chains. That is, 26 per cent of British Columbia's seine fleet is owned by big business. As many as 152 seiners and 83 gill-netters have converged on the central coast of British Columbia to catch Bella Coola River salmon. In some years and for some salmon stocks, the commercial fleet kills up to 90 per cent of all adult fish returning to spawn in the Bella Coola River.

The killing power of the commercial fleet is staggering. The average seiner boat has the capacity to store 34,000 kilograms of salmon; the average gill-net boat can hold 1800 kilograms of salmon. In 1992 an estimated 23,000 coho, 50,000 sockeye, 5 million pinks, 178,000 chum and 35,000 chinook salmon returned to the central coast, headed for the Bella Coola River.

Forty seiners fishing for only one day each could have killed the entire coho, sockeye, chum and chinook salmon runs. It is a wonder anything survives.

At the dawn of a new millennium, fisheries managers are faced with a dilemma similar to the one that faced big game managers at the turn of the last century. Do fisheries continue to let stocks be exterminated by a subsidized but highly efficient commercial fleet, or do they change the philosophy behind fishing? Is it better to sell fish for "sport," killing fewer and realizing greater economic returns, or to slaughter them for the market, at unsustainable levels, while subsidizing the industry?

Clearly it is time to take a hard look at the value of freshwater fishing and compare it with the value of commercial fishing. Studies show that commercial fishing is heavily subsidized by taxpayers. In 1986 the Canadian auditor general conducted a comprehensive value-for-money audit of the commercial fisheries on the Pacific coast. The average annual wholesale value of commercially caught Pacific salmon during a twelve-year period was $253 million dollars. The audit found that the Department of Fisheries and Oceans Pacific budget was $110 million a year. Add to that the costs of harvesting and processing (an estimated $130 million) and the total cost of harvesting Pacific salmon was $240 million—roughly equal to the value of the fish in the marketplace.

To qualify for unemployment insurance, a fisher needs ten weeks of fishing. In a typical year, there is only one work day a week for fishers, so the government equates a single day's fishing with an entire week's work. To get the maximum allowable unemployment insurance benefits, a fisher needs to bring in only $750 worth of fish. This means a commercial fisher can work just ten days a year, earn only $7500—and qualify for

$11,000 in unemployment benefits. Commercial fishers collect an estimated $60 million worth of unemployment insurance each year.

When unemployment insurance costs, subsidies on boat construction and the cost of various government programs are considered, Canadian taxpayers are actually paying commercial fishers to wipe out steelhead and other Pacific salmon stocks. Finding a way to catch the abundant stocks without killing endangered species is the great challenge facing the commercial fishery.

Sports fishers are not subsidized by the taxpayer, and they pay a lot more per fish caught. A recent study conducted for the provincial Ministry of Tourism estimated that sports angling makes a $1.4 billion contribution to the British Columbia economy each year. The study, by D.P.A. Group Inc., of Vancouver, found that $800 million is generated by the saltwater recreational fishery and $600 million by freshwater fishing. Economists confirm that the annual economic value of British Columbia's sports fishery exceeds $1 billion dollars, and they predict that there will be a 60 per cent increase in sports-fishing activity by the year 2005.

If sports fishing is to grow, however, better fishing opportunities will have to be made available. Although there is a popular misconception that a lot of people love to go fishing so much they don't care if they catch anything, in fact rivers that fail to produce decent catches are soon abandoned by anglers.

The demand for quality sports fisheries—such as the Dean River summer steelhead fishery—is especially high. Between June 1 and September 30, up to seventy anglers a day are fishing for steelhead on the Dean, which is located just north of the Bella Coola drainage. The river generates over $100,000 in direct licence sales every year. Over $1 million dollars is spent by the anglers on hotels, guides and floatplanes. Guided anglers are willing to pay $500 a day to fish the Dean. Best of all, the average taxpayer does not have to subsidize the killing of these fish—for all of the 3000 steelhead annually caught in the Dean are released. Studies show that less than 10 per cent will die, meaning the vast majority are able to spawn.

In contrast, commercial fishers on the central coast kill all the salmon they can. They get $1.50 to $2.00 a pound for chinook, $1.25 to $2.50 a pound for sockeye salmon, 15 cents to 25 cents a pound for pink salmon, 70 cents a pound for coho salmon, 65 cents a pound for bright chum salmon and 30 cents a pound for dark chum salmon. There is no market for steelhead, but some fishers launder them into their catch as chinook or take them home to smoke.

By some estimates, the commercial fleet catches from several hundred to several thousand Dean River steelhead each year. And the federal government sanctions this subsidized slaughter because the commercial fleet can't figure out a way to get salmon without killing steelhead.

For decades people have talked about shifting to in-river fisheries, where salmon are taken in weirs, the way the Natives traditionally fished, or in beach seines, where a net is drawn into a pond and salmon are selected, one at a time, to be either killed or released. Such techniques make sense—but there is such a state of political paralysis, brought on by a commercial industry that fears loss of profits as well as by timid governments, that virtually no progress has been made.

Although the federal fisheries department has tried to limit the killing of valuable sports fish, the state of steelhead, coho and chinook stocks tells the true story. Stocks are being driven into extinction, and still the commercial harvest continues.

Clearly, from an economic and an ecological perspective, it makes far more sense to promote recreational angling than it does to subsidize destructive commercial fishing. Not only should any commercial fishery that kills coho, chinook and steelhead be banned—but a reallocation of some sockeye should be made to promote sports fisheries in rivers such as the Bella Coola.

A ban on coho fishing introduced in some coastal areas in 1998 was a positive step, but it didn't go far enough. A bold move away from the indiscriminate slaughter of commercial fishing—a banning of gill nets and a return to weirs or fish traps—would result in vastly improved returns to our rivers and inshore waters. If salmon runs were at historical levels, an enormous, lucrative sports fishery would flourish, nutrient-poor watersheds would be refertilized—and Native fisheries, which have been wiped out in many areas, could be fully restored. Among other things, you would see steelhead runs reborn in the Bella Coola and hundreds of other rivers along the Pacific Coast.

Driving up through the verdant Bella Coola Valley, under towering snow-capped peaks, I pass beside farm fields where deer are browsing. A young buck lifts his head, tattered velvet hanging from one horn. Within days the first muffled rifle shots will be heard and deer like this one will vanish into the woods. In a field of stubble a red fox, ears on full alert, is hunting for voles amid ribbons of old hay. In another field a flock of fifty Canada geese jostles and honks as the birds graze on grass. In a nearby horse pasture two teenage boys, their blue jeans soaked to the knees, are scanning the ground as they search for Psilocybe mushrooms among splotches of dung. Unaware of what is happening around them in nature, they have become fixed on the one thing that is of value to them—a small brown mushroom with a powerful hallucinogenic punch. I can't understand why they seek phantasm, but they would probably say the same about my search for steelhead, a fish which at times seems no less delusional.

The old Nuxalk called the month of October Siqalxam, which means the Moon When Fern Root Is Gathered. The Native people did not have gardens but gathered their crops from a variety of sources. Instead of potatoes, tomatoes, carrots, apples and beans, the Nuxalk collected rose hips, kinnikinnick, salal berries and the roots of ferns, clover and silverweed.

October was also when many traditional Nuxalk medicinal plants were gathered and prepared. At one time, over seventy-five coastal plants were used for various medicinal purposes. Bella Coola Native people still use Labrador tea, devil's club, red alder and stinging nettle, some of which are potentially lethal.

Soon the land becomes steeper, the forest grows closer to the road, and I know I have passed into a wilder place. At Fisheries Pool the parking lot, once crowded with RVs and campers, now stands empty, as do all the roadside pullouts used by anglers along the Bella Coola. The watershed is deserted.

Stopping near a great boulder dropped long ago by the glaciers, I follow a trail to the Atnarko River that takes me deep into a forest of old-growth fir, hemlock and cedar. The path winds over a lush carpet of red-stemmed feathermoss and aptly named electrified cat's-tail moss. The sun streams through the forest canopy in great golden shafts. Small greyish-brown moths flutter through the tree branches, searching for places to lay their eggs and a Steller's jay appears out of the shadows to search through partially open conifer cones for seeds. The bird is as blue as the flame on a welder's torch. A hairy woodpecker is busy nearby hammering away at a pine cone with its hard, sharp beak. Once it is in shreds, the cone grudgingly surrenders its seeds.

A noisy flock of nomadic red crossbills invades the upper canopy, like a flock of parrots working its way through the jungle. They cling tightly to fir cones, letting out sharp *jip-jip* calls and working furiously. As I look up, I am showered by debris.

Beside the trail I notice a bright reddish-orange mushroom, covered with white, warty bumps. A circle of dead insects lies on the ground below. It is the fly agaric, the most deadly mushroom in the woods. It looks a lot like a budding pine mushroom, but if you eat it, it will cause spasms, delirium, drowsiness and coma.

I sniff the air and catch the musty odour of pine mushroom. After a fruitless search in the moss I glance up to see several hanging in tree branches. It's the winter stash of a red squirrel, and I leave it untouched.

I'm hot inside my waders when I finally make it to the river's edge, the clear water sparkling in the sunlight. There are grizzly bear tracks in the shore mud; a single line that wanders in and out of the water and then disappears up the bank into the forest. Most of the bears this time of day are resting in their beds on the side hills. Fishing season for them is almost over, and some grizzlies are already on their way back to denning areas as far away as Tanya Lake, the Blackwater River, the Klinaklinni River and the Ilgachuz Mountains. But a few still wander the river, looking for a last easy meal. All that remains of this year's salmon run are the scattered, dismembered carcasses of chinook, pink and chum salmon. The wrung-out carcasses consist mainly of skin and bones, and it is hard to imagine that the bears get much nutrition from them. (By the time November rolls around, bears will eat everything except the lower jaw, gills, gut and caudal fins.) A few bears still try for spawning coho, but most gorged themselves during the height of the run and are ready for hibernation. The bears have put on a thick, fatty layer, consuming up to 40,000 calories a day during the salmon harvest.

In the pools I see a few fall chum holding over their redds and the dark, restless shape of an occasional finning coho. In the water dead pink carcasses have collected in a pile. They are covered with a thick, grey, woolly film.

The river bottom is littered with pale orange eggs left over from the one million pink salmon that spawned this year in the Atnarko. It is a time of plenty for the resident rainbows, cutthroat and Dolly Varden and for the river's prolific insect population. I hear dippers singing somewhere among the stones, and I see a mature bald eagle drop from a large cottonwood tree to fly slowly downstream.

Stonefly casings are stuck on rocks near the faster water. Even this late in the year a few aquatic insects are hatching in the warm afternoon sun. A hatch of large grey mayflies is coming off, and a few fall caddis flies can be seen blundering across the surface. Reflecting against the bright sky backdrop are hundreds and hundreds of small black flies, rising and falling in a chaotic dance.

For the fly-fisher, the most productive pattern in October is a simple ball of orange that looks like a small cluster of salmon eggs. Trout feed heavily on the eggs, and steelhead will crush them in their mouths and then spit them out. For some unknown reason the summer-run steelhead that are holding in the river now are much more likely to feed than their late-fall, winter and spring counterparts. Up to 50 per cent of summer-run steelhead contain evidence of feed in their stomachs.

Egg imitations are not the only flies that work in the Atnarko in October. Trout and steelhead will also take large black stonefly imitations, muddler minnows, flies with strips of light-coloured rabbit fur that look like drifting pieces of salmon flesh—and large deer-hair dry flies.

My favourite technique is to first run a dry fly over a riffle and then, if repeated casts are refused, to dead-drift a weighted egg imitation or black stonefly nymph close to the bottom. I use a floating line and a 10-pound test leader, just in case a steelhead comes out of nowhere.

In this stretch of the Atnarko River the water flows quickly through a series of alternating rapids, riffles and pools. Unlike the lower end of the river, where there are large, slow pools, here there is plenty of choppy white water. The rainbows like to hold in the current where the riffle empties into the head of a pool, or at the tailout, where the current lifts food up from the bottom as it speeds to spill into the rapids below. Undercut banks, snags that trail in the water and pockets behind boulders in the middle of boiling, fast rapids are all worth exploring. The fish lie in the slower water near the bottom of the stream, and when they come up it is often with a dash that brings them through the surface in a splashy rise. Sometimes a trout will jump out, turn over in the air and come down on the fly.

Below me is 15 metres of frothy white riffle that runs under some overhanging logs on the opposite bank. In the shadows the water slows and deepens. Cedar branches lean out over the middle of the pool. It is the kind of place that a fly-fisher just knows will hold trout.

At the tailout a fallen cedar sticks out from the bank. Sunlight is shining on the broken tip of the tree, and a cloud of swarming midges dances just above it. Thousands of male midges are moving in unison, first up and then down, somehow all staying together. A breeze sets the swarm in a circular motion. The wind blows them slightly upstream, and then they regroup around the snag. Blundering past this delicate scene is a giant orange sedge with mottled brown wings that occasionally dips down to the water to release her eggs. Each time the fly stirs the surface, two or three juvenile steelhead dart excitedly after it. Halfway down the pool, a small rainbow jumps and takes it out of the air.

At nearly 5 centimetres long, the giant orange sedge is the largest caddis fly found on the coast of British Columbia. Like all caddis flies, the adults have two pairs of wings folded tentlike over the back when at rest. The body is yellowish-orange, and the legs are a brownish-yellow. Typically, adults emerge and mate and females lay eggs over a three- to four-week period in the fall. Unlike most caddis fly species, they are most active in the afternoon and evening just before sunset.

The fly I'd tied on had a dark brown deer-hair hackle and a rust-coloured body that perfectly matched the sedge. I hoped there were enough flies hatching to prime the fish. At times the giant orange sedge, like the giant stonefly, stirs the interest of the largest trout and the summer steelhead. I riffle-hitched the leader, looping it around the eye of the hook, so that it would be cocked at an angle on the surface, creating a wake when it skated over the tailout.

My first cast quarters across the current, and I follow the line down with my rod tip. When the fly is about a metre from a jumble of boulders in a deep slot, I let the fly swing across, creating a well-defined V as it plows across the surface. Nothing.

I wade a few steps, cast into the fast white water and watch the fly dance down to the seam of slower water at the head of the pool. In a rotating, smooth piece of river a fish suddenly bulges, pulling down the fly. Instinctively I strike, and a golden flash pulses in response, just under the surface. The fish turns away, hooked in the side of the jaw, jumps twice and then bulldogs straight upstream into rapids above me. The resident rainbows in the Atnarko are rarely more than half a kilogram or so, but they always seem bigger. They have a distinctive football shape that has earned them their nickname, slab-sides. The fish is quickly beaten and I slide it close to the shore. It is a classic slab-sided male rainbow about 38 centimetres long—and 7 to 10 centimetres thick. It weighs about half a kilogram. It takes only a second to remove the barbless hook, and the trout darts away.

About halfway down the rapids is a dark slot, lying beside several large stones, as green as moss. As the fly drifts over the dark water, a large fish suddenly rolls. It is too big to be a trout. I pause on the strike, allowing the fish to pull the fly under, and then gently tighten, dragging the hook into the corner of its mouth. The fish explodes, sending a shower of water across the pool as it turns to race downstream, with me running after it over the cobblestones. The rod is bent sharply, and the line goes from the reel in a blur. The fish charges through the tailout and down a fast run to the pool below. Forty-five metres gone, it jumps high, black in silhouette against the sunlit river. For a dreadful moment, it feels as if the fish has thrown the fly, but I strip in the slack line and feel it again, vibrating in the current. Five minutes later a beautiful 3-kilogram steelhead comes in. It is a buck, still quite silver, but with a splash of pink across its side. It could be a big trout but seems too streamlined to be an Atnarko slab-side. I release the fish with a simple twist of the fly. It lies for a moment in knee-deep water, its tail fanning steadily; then, with a flash, it is gone into the dark pool. I sit amid the river stones, my feet in the current, heart beating. I don't want another fish to crowd in on the image of the steelhead jumping like that, so I take down my rod, put the fly back in its box and made my way up the forest trail. There is a lot to think about and no need to hurry.

Summer steelhead are in trouble all across North America. In British Columbia alone, wild summer steelhead stocks are at less than half historical levels. It is estimated that commercial fishers are responsible for over 90 per cent of all adult summer steelhead deaths each year in British Columbia.

November

~

Moon of Dances

The rain falls gently on the black cottonwoods, rattling on every furled and mottled leaf, on every twig and gnarl of bark, so that the air hisses with a soft radio static. The lichens that drape the old branches glisten in yellow and silver. A gust of wind shakes the trees, and heavy drops spatter on the river below, breaking the mirrored images so that the reflected forest seems to pulse. Somewhere, far away in the estuary, on the edge of the sea, trumpeter swans are calling, and their voices are lifted and dispersed by the wind. No matter how cold the east wind blows in the months ahead, the birds will stay. They are home for the winter.

Ponds are freezing at night now and waterfalls are turning to ice high on the mountains. For the Nuxalk, this bleak month was a time for ceremonies; this was the Moon of Dances. They settled into their dark, smoky longhouses, rich with the smell of cedar and dried salmon, to wait for spring and celebrate their good fortune with pounding drums, chants and spectral dances, for they had been born into a world of plenty.

November is a time when most fly-fishers reluctantly put away their rods, sensing in the act a passing of time, for the season is over and the river is empty. But once, not so very long ago, you could fly-fish in the Bella Coola River late into November with a good chance of hooking a fresh-run steelhead, a fish so hard and clean it seemed carved from ice. This was the last run of the year, coming in from the dark Pacific under the cover of storm clouds, running up with showers of numbing rain while the Native villages slept and the forest lay silent. They were the most secretive and perhaps the most beautiful of all the salmon, and catching one would revitalize any tired soul. Over the past few decades, however, the number of late-running fish has declined dramatically. About four hundred used to arrive in November, moving quickly up from the estuary to hold in the upper Bella Coola and lower Atnarko. It is thought only a handful remain now.

The fall fish weren't just late-running summer fish; they were—and are, if they still exist—a distinct subspecies. They had riper eggs and heavier milt sacs than the earlier summer steelhead. They travelled more rapidly upstream and fed less than the earlier migrants. But they would take a fly—and when they did they fought wildly, as if ignited with the energy of an electrical storm. They had pale green backs and bright silver flanks tinged with pink. Their bellies were as white as swan down. They were stunningly attractive, and the promise of them made even the coldest days worth braving.

Not only has the late-fall run declined badly over recent years, but the Bella Coola itself has shown signs of deterioration. Each fall the river seems to flood a little faster, to become turbid when it once ran clear. After a heavy rainstorm, the Bella Coola blows out quickly, turning a dark brown. And those who have fished the river for the past twenty or thirty years say it takes a lot longer for the dirty water to settle. The silt that clouds the Bella Coola these days is not glacial flour, ground from the mountaintops, but rather it is rich topsoil, gritty and dark. It is eroded from a thousand cuts. Rivulets spring to life in the scars left by bulldozer blades, in the depressions made by backhoe tracks, in ditches scraped into the hillsides and from roadways trowelled through the earth by gigantic machines. Feeding into this intricate network of unintended canals, streams and watercourses are barren slopes, where logging has stripped away the forest.

Although the Bella Coola's upper watershed lies protected in Tweedsmuir Park, extensive logging has taken place in the lower valley and up many of the tributaries. The raw, zigzag road patterns show the forest industry's trail of relentless pursuit, and down those roads, when it rains, the mountains move.

As I drive up the main valley on a day that dawned clear and crisp after a night's rain, a convoy of three logging trucks suddenly rushes past, headed for Bella Coola. They send out an air blast that rocks my Toyota 4Runner. For a moment a whiff of spruce saturates the air, and then it is gone. In my rearview mirror I see the raw butt ends of the trunks, trailing from the last truck. A few branches stick up, like turkey feathers on a plucked fowl. Flecks of bark shower across the highway.

Logging in the Bella Coola Valley has a long history, but it is only in the last century that it evolved into an intense industrial activity that has done enormous environmental damage. Loggers and logging companies today are far more aware of the environment than they ever were, but they are also strictly efficient and their technological power is immense.

The Nuxalk were the first loggers. They used stone axes to cut the trees and cedar and rawhide ropes to drag the logs to the river. The logs were floated down to the villages, where they were used to build longhouses, dugout canoes and totems. In some places the loggers drove wedges into living trees to split out long planks. There are still dark groves on the north side of the river where you can walk on a thick moss carpet and see where they took out planks. The trunks are indented where the trees healed. Running through one grove of "culturally modified trees" is a deeply worn game trail and a small meandering brook, where coho fry flit for cover.

The Nuxalk used the inner bark of cedar to make clothing and fish nets; rough planks were used to build longhouses; baskets and rainhats were woven from the pliable roots of Sitka spruce. In ten thousand or more years the Nuxalk had no appreciable impact on the forest. They were part of it and it was part of them. It must also be noted that the Nuxalk lacked the technology to do any extensive logging, and the population was relatively small.

With the arrival of European settlers, things quickly changed. The first water-powered sawmills started operation in the late 1800s, and soon they were supplying high-grade lumber for houses, canneries and dock construction. But the forest seemed endless and what trees were taken hardly mattered.

The cut soon began to escalate, however. In the early 1900s, a pulp-and-paper mill was built at Ocean Falls, not far down the coast from Bella Coola. To supply demand, more and more trees were taken from the rich, old-growth forest in the Bella Coola Valley. Trees were cut adjacent to the river and floated down to the estuary, where they were held in log rafts until sold. In the forest you can still see the stumps from the first pass—some of them so broad that you could set a dining room table on them. Over the years several major logging companies began to operate on the central coast and the cut continued to grow. The forest was soon being cut far faster than it could regrow—a practice that continues to this day.

Logging is big business in the Bella Coola Valley and surrounding central coast, which exports about $300 million worth of wood each year. But precious little of that wealth is returned to the community of Bella Coola, where only about 150 people are directly employed in the industry. In this small village, which is located in one of the most beautiful valleys in the world, the schools are falling apart, there are next to no recreational facilities, water and sewer systems are corroding, and there is massive unemployment—perhaps as high as 80 per cent. Drug and alcohol abuse is not uncommon. The government claims to have no money to correct these problems, and the logging companies donate relatively little to community projects. And yet local people say almost nothing in protest as the mountains around them are denuded. Indeed, when environmental groups, including Greenpeace, invaded the area in 1997 to protest logging, many locals angrily criticized them as outsiders or dismissed them as "tree-huggers," demanding that they leave the valley.

Each year roughly ninety thousand trees are cut from the shrinking old-growth forest in the Bella Coola watershed. Some are a thousand years old. A procession of 3500 logging trucks is needed to remove them all.

You need only drive up a side valley to see the impact of modern logging. Clayton Falls Creek once ran beneath a towering green canopy; it pooled and licked its way to the sea. Now it vaults through a clear-cut, unshaded and unprotected.

A typical coastal salmon stream has clean, well-oxygenated

water flowing through it year-round. A dense growth of stream-side vegetation shelters the water, filters the rain, guards the stream banks from erosion and provides cover for fish. The leaves and nettles that fall into the stream are food for aquatic insects, which in turn feed juvenile fish. Nearly 70 per cent of the nutrients and total energy supplied to juvenile salmon ultimately comes from terrestrial sources. The surrounding forest, then, is not separate from the stream but is part of it.

Clear-cut logging strips away the cover—often right to the stream edge. Soil is exposed, and in many areas it is compacted by machinery. Normally rain is intercepted by trees, by millions of leaves, by hanging beards of lichen, by bark and countless needles, by underlying layers of vegetation, litter and soil. Until all these layers are saturated, only a small fraction of rain seeps into the streams. After logging, the rain sluices directly off the hills, carrying soil, rocks, leaves and branches with it. The debris crashes down slope and stream banks collapse. Not surprisingly, floods are more common in coastal streams that have been clear-cut. Studies have shown that coho fry production is a function of the stability of water flows. The more floods, the fewer fish.

About 25 kilometres east of Bella Coola the Salloomt River pours down a steep valley, crashing from one rocky pocket of water to the next. To get to the mouth of the river, you drive up the Bella Coola Valley, past Hagensborg, turn north to cross the Bella Coola and then double back until you reach a bridge over the noisy Salloomt. Just downstream you can see where the small river, with a lick and a swirl, enters the main river. A trail leads through the woods to where the waters join. My breath rises like mist as I set out, the fly line slapping against my rod with each step. Most of the leaves have fallen from the alders, birch and other deciduous trees that grow in profusion along the path. In the bare branches I can see some of the nests birds have made, using lichen, spiderwebs, grass, the down from their own breasts and seed thistles. Suspended between a fork, far out on the branch of an alder is the delicate nest of a warbling vireo. In a fork in the trunk of a willow shrub, about half a metre off the ground, is the tiny, compact, cup-shaped nest of a yellow warbler. I kneel to examine it. The outer part of the nest is made of dried yellow grass and shredded red cedar, neatly woven together. You can't help but wonder if this is where the Nuxalk first got the idea of weaving bark to create clothes and baskets. Higher up in an alder is the bulky stick nest of a crow, solid and utilitarian. I walked past this site a dozen times last spring, unaware of the silent, nesting birds that were just a few metres away.

A week ago, the Salloomt River ran clear and low, but now the rains have turned the water brown. Visibility in the Bella Coola River has dropped as well, as the tributaries blow mud into the main river.

A few weeks earlier, the riverbanks were littered with the remains of thousands of rotting chum and pink salmon. But now all that remains are a few gill covers, broken fragments of vertebrae, the occasional salmon tail and raglike pieces of skin caught on snags. Scavengers and a few autumn freshets have swept most of the dead away.

From the mouth of Salloomt I can see where the Nooklikonnik, Snootli and Thorsen Creeks all flow down to join the Bella Coola. The side valleys are all steep. Snow covers the upper mountains, folding down to just below the dark tree line. Braids of water flow into the blackness of the forest. In the lower part of the valleys, the old clear-cuts look ragged and grey because of the bare branches of the deciduous trees. Soon they will be deep in snow and the erosion will stop. Until spring.

The Salloomt River, like many of the other lower-valley streams, has undergone great changes over the years. At one time there was a run of Salloomt steelhead, a run of Salloomt chinook and an early August run of large Salloomt sea-run cutthroat. Except for a handful of fish, those runs are all gone now.

The steelhead that returned to this once vibrant river arrived in April through June, and they could often be seen just below the logging bridge. Up to a hundred steelhead could be counted in a drift, but the usual size of the run was fewer than thirty fish. The chinook came up in May and June, matured in deep lower-river pools and spawned around September.

The Salloomt cutthroat were large trout that typically weighed 1 or 2 kilograms. They had a distinctive yellow-green colour. They came into the river in early August and stayed until they spawned the following spring. Local fly-fishers say they haven't seen those fish for at least ten years, so they are either extinct or so few as to be invisible.

The reasons given for the decline of the Salloomt's runs are familiar. The pink salmon commercial fishery is suspected of wiping out the sea-run cutthroat. The cutthroat migrated with the Atnarko pinks and were just the right size to get tangled in the commercial nets. Local sports anglers killed their share of fish, and logging had an untold impact on the Salloomt's spawning beds. Logging of the lower Salloomt River began in 1951 and continued into the late 1960s. Trees were cut from the river edge far up onto the hillsides. After the lower valley was logged, cutting moved farther upstream, where it is still taking place. For more than forty years, muck has been pouring into the river. As I wade out to cast, the silt from a distant slope washes around my boots, and they soon disappear in a swirl of brown water.

Perhaps to suit the mood as much as to match the hatch, I tie on a small white fly that imitates the maggots that can be found feeding on rotting salmon carcasses. An egg fly would work just as well, because coho are still spawning in the tributaries and the cutthroat are watching for roe rolling past in the current. But somehow the white fly selects itself. It happens that way.

Within an hour, two small but firm cutthroat have come to hand and been released, and two other fish have tugged gently at the fly but were missed. Then the river grows quiet and I stand for a long time, my line trailing down into the dark water. I have come to take the pulse of the river with a line as thin as a strand of cedar bark, and the heartbeat has never seemed so faint.

December

Moon When the Sun Rests

A heavy, wet snow has fallen during the night, spreading a humped white blanket across the estuary. Here and there clumps of tired blonde grass push through. A flock of mallards bursts from a tidal channel, scattering snow crystals in the air like pollen. Far out on the flats a drift of trumpeter swans stirs and shifts as an eagle circles overhead. Along the river, as the morning warms, clumps of snow drop from the tree branches, vanishing as they become water. The snow eats the sound of the river as it passes over its stone bed; it eats the sound of the forest.

Driving up the highway, travelling east from Bella Coola, I set out on the last fishing trip of the year. Somehow I know that today I will find a steelhead that is buried somewhere in the river, its heart beating like a drum. In the back of the truck I can hear the tip of my fly rod tapping against the window as it picks up the vibrations of the road. It seems to be chattering with anticipation. Every fishing trip starts with a sense of optimism, but sometimes there is a deeper level of certainty, a predator's instinct that comes from a vision of a steelhead rising through layers of green water to take your fly. I have seen steelhead stand on their heads to pluck one of my flies from the bottom, and I have seen them tilt up to take a floating dry fly with an audible snap of their jaws. I have seen them rise, head, dorsal, tail, and I have seen deep, slow glints of silver, far away, as they twisted sideways in the current. I have taken them unseen too, by intuition, striking for no apparent reason, but finding a fish there.

The dream I have now, however, is of a fish and a rise form that I have never seen. The steelhead materializes over a bed of mossy stones; it rises on a steady diagonal line to intercept my fly, which glows like an orange spark. The river that divides and joins us seems to be made of sheets of tinted glass, which rotate slowly. When the fish takes the fly, the dream ends. I know that to finish the dream I must find the steelhead, and I know that the steelhead is somewhere in the Bella Coola River, waiting for me, as it has been all year.

Few people fish the river in December (Siimt) anymore. There used to be a small but strong run of steelhead in the twelfth month, a continuation of the November run, but that stock, like all the others, has dwindled to a point where it is not really worth going out. Still, some do fish and one, I know, found steelhead this week. A Nuxalk spin fisherman told me, in the quiet way that anglers will sometimes share the most precious information, that he'd just taken a fresh steelhead in a pool known as the Classic.

"Nice fish," he said. "Big. Silver as chrome." He held his rough hands far apart. And when he put his hands down the steelhead was gone.

I knew he'd killed the fish, exercising his Native right, and that was troubling. But I appreciated the information, which needn't have been shared and which didn't appear to be in general circulation, at least not yet. It jarred me out of my lethargy, and on a cold day with clouds as grey as salmon backs hanging over the mountains, I set out. In search of a wild steelhead.

Passing up through the farming district, I saw houses steepled in snow, smoke rising warmly from their chimneys. Trucks and cars were safely parked in driveways, covered with a 10-centimetre-thick blanket of fresh snow. The crops were long in and for most people there was no reason to go out. They were content to wait, knowing that sooner or later rain would come to wash the roads clear.

A highways crew had been through, plowing the main highway. Here and there I slowed to avoid hitting flocks of purple finches that were feeding on road salt. They rose up before me and settled back once I had passed. In thickets along the ditches I saw the flash of evening grosbeaks and common redpolls as they feasted on the tiny seeds inside birch cones. Occasionally, in the depth of winter, there will be an eruption of birds in the valley, as cold weather or poor feeding conditions on the Chilcotin Plateau push flocks down to the coast. Sometimes a weather front will move snowy owls down from the north, and they will sit along the field margins, startlingly visible in the dark green trees. Sometimes you can see them, white birds gliding over white fields in search of invisible mice, voles and shrews that are busy tunnelling under the snow cover. Owls hear rather than see the small mammals and dive, like ospreys into water, to take their prey. Sometimes you will see the long brush strokes their great wings have left in the snow.

The Classic Pool is more than 48 kilometres from Bella Coola, and it is nearly noon by the time I turn off the highway onto the Talchako forest road. There is no reason to fish early in

December; it is better to wait for the day to warm a little and, one hopes, give the steelhead a reason to stir. The gravel road is layered in ice and deeply rutted. I shift to low four-wheel drive and slither along, the undercarriage of my truck scraping on the snow ridge between the deep tire tracks. I cross the Bella Coola River, running smooth and dark, turn east again and after several kilometres find a spot to park. There is no trail visible, but I know if I work my way through a clump of small firs, aiming for a grove of old growth in the distance, I will find a route through a slough to the river.

I slip down the steep bank next to the logging road and push through the wet undergrowth, knocking clumps of snow off the branches. My breath is steamy and heavy with moisture. Except for the crunching of my boots, the forest is silent. Then, just a rod length away, a ruffed grouse leaps into the air, its wings drumming hard against its breast, snow flying. It soars and tilts off through the trees, leaving an exit hole in the snowbank where it had spent the night. Grouse, ptarmigan and even redpolls routinely bury themselves in snow, flying right into a drift, where they settle for the night—waiting to startle unwary travellers.

Tracks of snowshoe hares lace through the thickets, and twisting among them are delicate ribbons of deer mice footprints. Snowshoe hares sustain many predators, including wolves, foxes, cougars, lynx, hawks and owls. In a single winter up to 40 per cent of the hare population is eaten by its hunters. Hares are prolific breeders, but their population rises and falls in a six- to twelve-year cycle. At one time lynx were blamed for declines in snowshoe hare numbers, but studies have shown that the availability of food is a more important factor. Too many hares will overgraze their habitat, leading to starvation and a crash in the population. Not surprisingly, when snowshoe hare populations drop, lynx numbers decline soon afterwards. Over time the vegetation recovers, the hare population builds, and there is food again for the predators. It may be that ancient humans were once caught up in a similar rhythm, but now when a game or fish population declines, the number of people just keeps on increasing.

The deep snow is hard going, and it's a relief when I finally get down to flat ground and into the grove of old-growth trees. The snow is not so heavy under the dark canopy, and the well-worn trails cut by deer show I'm not the only one to find the walking much easier. A movement catches my eye, and I see a herd of about ten mule deer, frozen in the shadows. Their reddish-brown coats of summer have been replaced by thick, grey winter fur. One of the bucks has a single antler on its head and, compared with the does around him, is quite thin. When I stop, they all bound away, vanishing with surprising ease. The deer have penned here for the winter to feed on twigs blown down from the tops of the Douglas firs and on the yellow lichens that fall from upper branches. It is hard to believe that lichens can support deer, but research has found the beardlike plant is vital to their survival. The lichen only flourishes on old-growth trees.

There's the soft outline of a path through the woods now, one first made by animals but since expanded by anglers, and it takes me upstream through another 45 metres of old-growth cedar and spruce. At the base of one tree is a spattering of blood and a pile of ruffed grouse feathers. I look up to see a marten dart for cover, dragging its limp prey with it.

Beyond the old growth I pass again into a logged area, where the snow is thick and I have to scramble over debris. Then I walk through a stately grove of black cottonwood and cross a frozen bog, where the ground is lumpy and slippery. A beaver lodge, steeped in snow, with a wisp of warm air streaming up from inside, sits in the middle of a frozen pond. The farmer is home from the field.

I tread carefully on the ice, testing to see if it will crack, and then half-skate, half-walk to the far side. Finally, I push through a thicket of hemlock and break out onto the banks of the Bella Coola River. The walk has taken only about thirty minutes, but it seemed much longer. I unzip the neck of my jacket to let cool air pour in. The sky has begun to open up, and sunlight is shining through a large break in the clouds for the first time in days. I can see a smattering of blue. The air is a few degrees warmer than the river, and there's mist rising off the water; it swirls up in spirals and seems to catch in the thick branches of red cedars.

A gentle current flows into the head of the Classic Pool, refracting light over a shallow, sand-and-gravel bottom, giving the water a golden colour. Along the far bank the water turns dark green as it grows deeper. The bows of overhanging trees, some still trimmed with snow, reflect on the surface. It is so quiet I hear the gentle surfacing of a fish near the head of the pool and turn to see the back and tail of a coho going down, its air bladder refilled. The last of the coho are spawning now, and the salmon are dark and exhausted. I wouldn't fish for them.

There aren't any tracks in the fresh snow, but at the top of the run the pure blanket of whiteness is marred by a smudge. I push back the cover with my boot. This is where the steelhead was killed. All that remains is the stain of frozen blood. There are eagle prints around it and the strokes left by pinion feathers. Lumpy, under last night's snowfall, are the angler's tracks.

The winter steelhead are the last adult fish of the year to return to the Bella Coola River. They hold in the deeper, slow-moving pools of the upper river until spring runoff raises the Atnarko; then they move again, to spawning grounds far upstream.

Winter steelhead are said to be the most challenging of all of British Columbia's freshwater game fish to hook on the fly. The Bella Coola winter steelhead are no exception. To be successful, you need not only skill but the right water conditions, and you need to know exactly where the fish lie. You also need a little luck. More often than not it is too cold, it is raining too hard, the water is too high, or it is too muddy. When it gets too cold, a sheet of ice forms along the river's edge and islands of slush drift in the current. It's dangerous to walk along the shore, and the floating ice makes it impossible to control a fly line.

Today conditions are perfect. Snow lines the bank, but there's no ice shelf and I can easily wade into the river. I sense the steelhead are lying in the deep water along the far bank, in the shadow of the forest.

When steelhead find a lie they hold hour after hour, day after day, barely moving. It must be strange for such powerful, active fish to become almost comatose. But their main function now is to conserve energy, while their eggs or sperm ripen. They won't spawn until next March.

The cold water slows their metabolism, making it less likely they'll go for a fly. Bait fishers, who drift balls of sticky salmon eggs along the bottom, even have trouble at times and know they'll have to put their lure within 30 centimetres or so of a steelhead before it will take. A fly must be within centimetres, and even then it may be ignored.

The water is so clear I can see pebbles on the bottom 3 metres away. I tie on a long, slender leader. I choose a small egg fly, barely big enough to cover a fingernail. It will look like a single coho egg, drifting in the current, and I hope a steelhead will take it in the tip of its mouth.

Edging out into the current, my boots feeling their way over the smooth, cold stones, I start to cast gently across the river. I fish the fly at a dead drift, retrieve it quietly and cast again. Every few casts I take three steps down and repeat the process. I work the fly far out. In what seems like moments, an hour passes. I have become as mesmerized as the steelhead themselves, and time has become as fluid as the river. I cast and breathe and step down. The forest surrounds me as the waters of the Bella Coola surround the fish.

An invisible rectangle exists in space and time, encompassing the river and the stones and history. I have been searching for it in a dark forest, along an endless shoreline. Without knowing, I step inside. I am at one corner and the great, sleeping salmon is at the other. The line drifts between the opposing points.

I do not see the steelhead rise, but on this day I do not have too. I have seen it in my dream, so when it comes, I know. Suddenly in the middle of a cast that is exactly like a thousand before it, I sense the fish is on. I drive the rod up—and it bends hard. I feel a head shaking, deep in the river; it is powerful and slow, as if the steelhead is awakening under the weight of a glacier. I catch my breath, I hear my heart drumming like a grouse, I see the red blood on the snow, I know that somewhere river mist curls from the mouth of a running wolf and that great white swans are leaning forward to plunge their heads into the rich mud of the estuary. I know that the coho are moving gently together, shifting the stones, and I can hear salmon eggs falling. I know that the river glints like sunlight on the wings of a dipper and that night folds itself over the valley like the soft brown wings of a sedge. I hear the Nuxalk drummers, but their song falls like snow into the river and becomes silent. Everything is water.

Then the fish runs. It goes up along the far bank, the line hissing as it cuts through the reflection of the trees; then it dives under the swirling current at the head of the pool and runs, fast as a frightened deer, back down my side of the river. I strip line frantically, throwing loops up into the snow. The fish goes all the way to the tail of the pool, and the line I have regained shoots out through my hand. Bits of ice rattle in the guides like salmon teeth. The fight lasts an eternity but is over in moments, as if it somehow never existed. Finally I see the steelhead, its dark green back darker than the river stones. Its belly like snow. The blush of sunset on its cheeks. At some moment the fish and I agree the fight is done. It yields, is drawn miraculously towards me, an enormous fish of 6 or 7 kilograms, coming without a struggle, its perfectly formed body moving without friction. It seems cut from steel and polished by time. I kneel in the water and draw the steelhead against my legs, not believing a fish so powerful can suddenly be so submissive.

And then I see that it's bleeding.

As the gill plates move, clouds of rust billow from the fish of steel, ocher threads trail off in the water, marking the hidden currents.

I feel my centre give way.

A fish that bleeds will almost certainly die, for its wound will not congeal in the coldness of the river. I trace my hand up the leader, find the small hook, push it free from where it's embedded, deep in the mouth at the base of the tongue. When the fly comes out it is covered with a dark glob of blood. My hand is red, and later I will realize that I am bleeding too, that I have cut a finger on the steelhead's teeth.

I let the fish go and it rests in the shallows next to me. In that moment I sense the timelessness of nature and the fatalism of the spawning run. I know that the rivers I love are paved with the bones of the fish that I love and by this I am bound to the planet. The dazed steelhead stirs, its tail roiling the surface of the great Bella Coola River, and then it swims out, vanishing under the sheltering forest.

Field Notes

MONTHS OF PEAK FISH RETURNS
TO THE BELLA COOLA RIVER

March—First run of steelhead; eulachon

June—Chinook

July—Sockeye

August—Second run of steelhead; summer chum and pink
salmon

September—First run of coho and sea-run cutthroat

October—Second run of coho, fall chum and sea-run Dolly
Varden

November—Third run of steelhead

MONTHS OF PEAK SPAWNING

May—Steelhead, resident rainbows, cutthroat

August—Summer chum

September—Chinook, pink, sockeye, fall chum

October—Whitefish

November—Coho and Dolly Varden

December—Coho

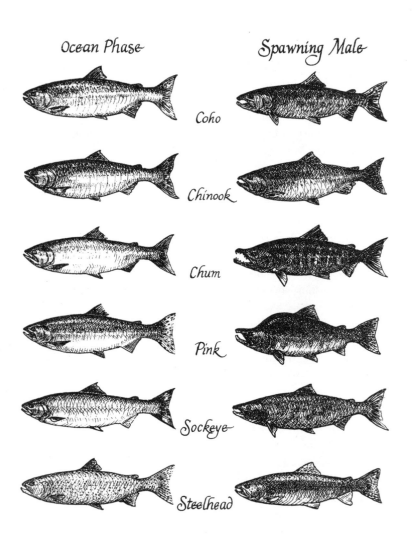

Ocean Phase

Spawning Male

Coho

Chinook

Chum

Pink

Sockeye

Steelhead

(partial list)

Blue mayfly (*Paraleptophlebia vaciva*)

Slate-cream mayfly (*Epeorus Iron albertae*)

Medium blue mayfly (*Epeorus Iron longimanus*)

Western quill Gordon (*Epeorus Ironopsis grandis*)

Western March brown (*Rithrogena hageni* & *Rithrogena robusta*)

Little blue-wing olive (*Baetis bicaudatus*)

Western green drake (*Drunella doddsi*)

Small western green drake (*Drunella flavilinea* & *Drunella spinifera*)

Pale morning mayfly (*Ephemerella inermis* & *Ephemerella infrequens*)

Small western dark hendrickson (*Serratella tibialis*)

Slate-winged mahogany mayfly (*Paraleptophlebia debilis*)

Medium brown and yellow stoneflies (*Kogotus nonus*; *Megarcys subtruncata*; *Rickera sorpta*)

Little green and yellow stonefly (*Kathroperla perdita*; *Paraperla frontalis*; *Swelta coloradensis*)

Little black stonefly (*Capniidae*)

Big golden stonefly (*Hesperoperla pacifica*)

Little sister sedge (*Cheumatopsyche* spp.)

Spotted sedge (*Hydropsyche* spp.)

Microcaddis (*Agraylea saltesea*)

Little plain brown sedge (*Lepidostoma roafi*)

Scaly wing sedge (*Ceraclea cancellata*)

Black dancer (*Mystacides alafimbriata*)

Long horn sedge (*Oecetis inconspicua*)

Pale western stream sedge (*Chyranda centralis*)

Summer flier sedge (*Limnephilus* spp.)

Little western dark sedge (*Oligophleboides sierra*)

Trees of the Bella Coola area

Sitka spruce (*Picea sitchensis*)
Western red cedar (*Thuja plicata*)
Yellow cedar (*Chamaecyparis nootkatensis*)
Douglas fir (*Pseudotsuga menziesii ssp. menziesii*)
Western hemlock (*Tsuga heterophylla*)
Black cottonwood (*Populus balsamifera ssp. trichocarpa*)
Paper birch (*Betula papyrifera*)
Lodgepole pine (*Pinus contorta var. latifolia*)
Amabilis fir (*Abies amabilis*)
Pacific yew (*Taxus brevifolia*)
Trembling aspen (*Populus tremuloides*)

Edible wild berries and fruits of the Bella Coola area

Alaskan blueberry (*Vaccinium alaskaense*)
Black cap raspberry (*Rubus leucodermis*)
Black currant (*Ribes hudsonianum*)
Bog cranberry (*Vaccinium oxycoccos*)
Crowberry (*Empetrum nigrum*)
Evergreen huckleberry (*Vaccinium ovatum*)
Highbush-cranberry (*Viburnum edule*)
Juniper (*Juniperus communis*)
Kinnikinnick (*Arctostaphylos uva-ursi*)
Black huckleberry (*Vaccinium membranaceum*)
Oval-leaved blueberry (*Vaccinium ovalifolium*)
Red elderberry (*Sambucus racemosa*)
Red huckleberry (*Vaccinium parvifolium*)
Salal (*Gaultheria shallon*)
Salmonberry (*Rubus spectabilis*)
Saskatoon berry (*Amelanchier alnifolia*)

FIELD NOTES

Thimbleberry (*Rubus parviflorus*)
Trailing black currant (*Ribes laxiflorum*)
Pacific crab apple (*Malus fusca*)
Wild gooseberry (*Ribes divaricatum*)
Red raspberry (*Rubus idaeus*)
Wild Nootka rose (*Rosa nutkana*)
Wild strawberry (*Fragaria virginiana*)

SUMMER RESIDENT BIRDS

Marbled murrelet (*Brachyramphus marmoratus*)
Red-breasted sapsucker (*Sphyrapicus ruber*)
Northern flicker (*Colaptes auratus*)
Red-winged blackbird (*Agelaius phoeniceus*)
Winter wren (*Troglodytes troglodytes*)
Robin (*Turdus migratorius*)
Varied thrush (*Ixoreus naevius*)
Song sparrow (*Melospiza melodia*)
Merlin (pigeon hawk) (*Falco columbarius*)
Kestrel (sparrow hawk) (*Falco sparverius*)
Red-tailed hawk (*Buteo jamaicensis*)
Yellow-rumped warbler (*Dendroica coronata*)
Ruby crowned kinglet (*Regulus calendula*)
Violet-green swallow (*Tachycineta thalassina*)
Orange-crowned warbler (*Vermivora celata*)
Tree swallow (*Tachycineta bicolor*)
Northern rough-winged swallow (*Stelgidopteryx serripennis*)
Brown-headed cowbird (*Molothrus ater*)
Lincoln's sparrow (*Melospiza lincolnii*)
Rufous hummingbird (*Selasphorus rufus*)
Hermit thrush (*Catharus guttatus*)
Band-tailed pigeon (*Columba fasciata*)

Barn swallow (*Hirundo rustica*)

Cliff swallow (*Hirundo pyrrhonota*)

Savannah sparrow (*Passerculus sandwichensis*)

Townsend's solitaire (*Myadestes townsendi*)

Yellow warbler (*Dendroica petechia*)

Wilson's warbler (*Wilsonia pusilla*)

Common yellowthroat warbler (*Geothlypis trichas*)

Pacific slope flycatcher (*Empidonax difficilis*)

Townsend's warbler (*Dendroica townsendi*)

MacGillivray's warbler (*Oporornis tolmiei*)

Black-throated gray warbler (*Dendroica nigrescens*)

Hammond's flycatcher (*Empidonax hammondii*)

Red-eyed vireo (*Vireo olivaceus*)

Vaux's swift (*Chaetura vauxi*)

Olive-sided flycatcher (*Contopus borealis*)

Cedar waxwing (*Bombycilla cedrorum*)

Solitary vireo (*Vireo solitarius*)

Spotted sandpiper (*Actitis macularia*)

Warbling vireo (*Vireo gilvus*)

Black-headed grosbeak (*Pheucticus melanocephalus*)

Western tanager (*Piranga ludoviciana*)

Alder flycatcher (*Empidonax alnorum*)

Western wood pewee (*Contopus sordidulus*)

Black swift (*Cypseloides niger*)

Kingbird (*Tyrannus* spp.)

Swainson's thrush (*Catharus ustulatus*)

Common nighthawk (*Chordeiles minor*)

American redstart (*Setophaga ruticilla*)

Dusky flycatcher (*Empidonax oberholseri*)

Year-round residents

American crow (*Corvus brachyrhynchos*)
Steller's jay (*Cyanocitta stelleri*)
Chestnut-backed chickadee (*Parus rufescens*)
Golden-crowned kinglet (*Regulus satrapa*)
Ruffed grouse (*Bonasa umbellus*)
Pileated woodpecker (*Dryocopus pileatus*)
Brown creeper (*Certhia americana*)
Great horned owl (*Bubo virginianus*)
Barred owl (*Strix varia*)
Great gray owl (*Strix nebulosa*)
Bald eagle (*Haliaeetus leucocephalus*)
Great blue heron (*Ardea herodias*)

Visitors

American widgeon (*Anas americana*)
Chipping sparrow (*Spizella passerina*)
Osprey (*Pandion haliaetus*)
Mountain bluebird (*Sialia currucoides*)
Golden-crowned sparrow (*Zonotrichia atricapilla*)
White-crowned sparrow (*Zonotrichia leucophrys*)
Pectoral sandpiper (*Calidris melanotos*)
Western sandpiper (*Calidris mauri*)
Lesser golden-plover (*Pluvialis dominica*)
Northern shoveler (*Anas clypeata*)
Water pipit (*Anthus spinoletta*)
Northern harrier (marsh hawk) (*Circus cyaneus*)
California gull (*Larus californicus*)
Bonaparte's gull (*Larus philadelphia*)
American white pelican (*Pelecanus erythrorhynchos*)

BIRD DENSITY IN LOGGED VERSUS UNLOGGED OLD GROWTH,
IN PAIRS, PER 100 HECTARES, AVERAGED FROM SEVERAL
STUDIES DEALING WITH LARGE AREAS OF FOREST

	Logged	Unlogged
Golden-crowned kinglet	1	67
Townsend's warbler	4	36
Hermit thrush	4	29
Brown creeper	1	43
Red-breasted nuthatch	14	35